Bathroom Planning & Design

With Perspective Drawing Essentials

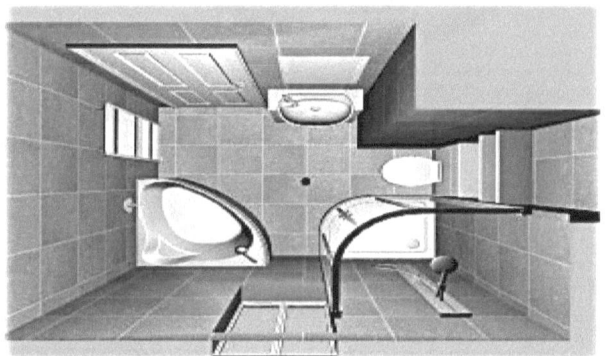

Copyright

this is dedicated to all those delegates with blank expressions on their face as they tried to grasp the intricacies of Bathroom Planning before they even got familiar with kitchen planning.

2

Bathrom Planning & Design

Perhaps they didn't want to be there at all but I am sure they all went out and became excellent kitchen and bathroom planners During our live training sessions we were always somewhat surprised about how frightened most delegates were about planning bathrooms for sale. Most delegates had and have little experience about plumbing and a lot of installers seem to want to keep the knowledge to themselves.

You need to have a rapport with your installer unless you are only planning safe simple bathrooms - virtually a one for one replacement. Unfortunately this is rarely the case as the majority of buyers now want a proper shower facility often as wel as a bath. However most reasonably new houses have a bathroom and an en suite which is usually a shower room so it is far less complicated than before. The complication arises when the customer wants you to plan and brand new extended bathroom or have set aside a different room and want you to convert this new room to a really grandiose bathroom.

1

Introduction

This is our latest paperback, produced in a popular portrait version which can contain more pages than our usual landscape publishings and in monochrome this means we can keep the price as low as possible.

Now you can purchase the very best perspective book money can buy plus the most experienced and knowledgable Bathroom design guide ever produced: This comes fro, years of practical experience and correcting the errors of hundreds of DIY market delegates eager to get it right.

This contrasts markedly with the snooty delegates fro, the Bathroom Boutiques who weren`t interested in getting it right just in making the best impression.

That is where the problem starts because you are then working within the limitations of the installer. Unless you are a supply and fit operation you will need to try and get to grips with the installer's knowledge and limitations. There are many small bore systems these days but have their own complications and remember they generate noise - not everyone's cup of tea. So we shall start our studies by looking at the essential rules of Bathroom Planning, some product details, a bit of plumbing and of course, ergonomic and anthropometric considerations

What is the definitios of ERGONOMICS

"the study of people's efficiency in their working environment."

What is the Definition of Anthropometry

"anthropometry, especially as it relates to the design of furniture and machinery."

The study of the human body and its movement. Perhaps these illustration can suggest to the planner that it is important to take into account the physical attributes of the end user. Clearly a 5 foot nothing housewife is not going to be very keen don 900 high wall units.

Similarly if there are a number of children in the house some or all of them may be working in the kitchen from time to time. For example if the sink is heavily used for dishwashing and in particular fresh vegetable preparation there may be a case for using either a continental style worktop height or a dropped zone in this area. If you are using a dropped sink zone then it would appear logical to adopt a dropped hob zone as well.

Electrics already have their requirements for accessibility of the height of switches and sockets but again there may be a case to take extra care when making extensive electric variations and installations to ensure that switching heights and socket positions are ideal for the household and not just for the house. You may have designed a wonderful lighting plan but if nobody can reach the switches it is wasted.

We covered most of the ergonomic and an-

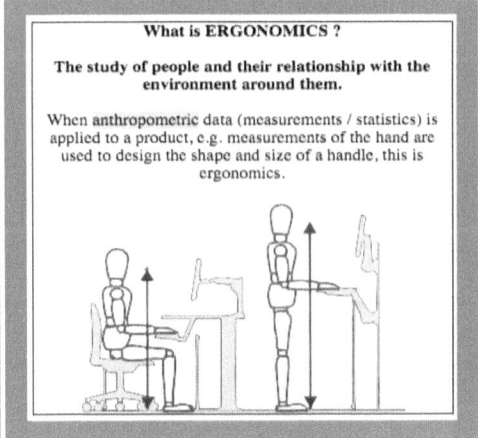

What is ERGONOMICS ?

The study of people and their relationship with the environment around them.

When anthropometric data (measurements / statistics) is applied to a product, e.g. measurements of the hand are used to design the shape and size of a handle, this is ergonomics.

thropometric issues in the Kitchen Planning guide but many of you will not have seen this and so we have repeated a lot of the detail but have added some of the important issues that apply purely to bathrooms.

Spacing in a bathroom can be quite critical and there are many planning and spacing errors.

A lot of the issues are pretty obvious and frankly should not have been made but often planners do not think things through carefully and many planners cannot visualise the space with appliances in situ.

One of the issues that clearly affects the comfortable use of bathrooms is the comfort zones that should be applied. There used to be British Standards as to how to relate these spaces but they have been a little lost in the space of time. Some of the issues are obvious e.g. space infront of the bath to dry yourself. Height of grab rails and yet many guides are simply not correct. Space inside a shower enclosure. Again the designer specifies a silly size to suit the room and the content but not necessarily the 19 stone husband who probably is not going to fit inside a 700mm square enclosure.

I think we have all been guilty of placing a shower fitting too high for a child to reach or perhaps the 5foot nothing lady of the house? Mind you how do you equate a 6'3" man of the house with his 5' spouse. Probably by specifying a Grand riser with fixed head and flexible hose but with a slider rail not just a hook?

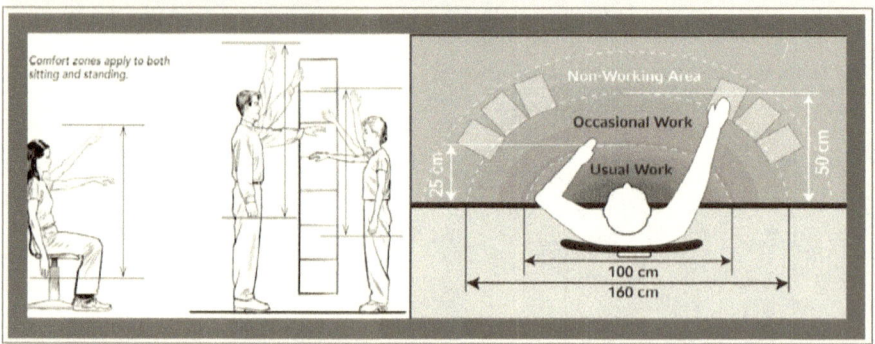

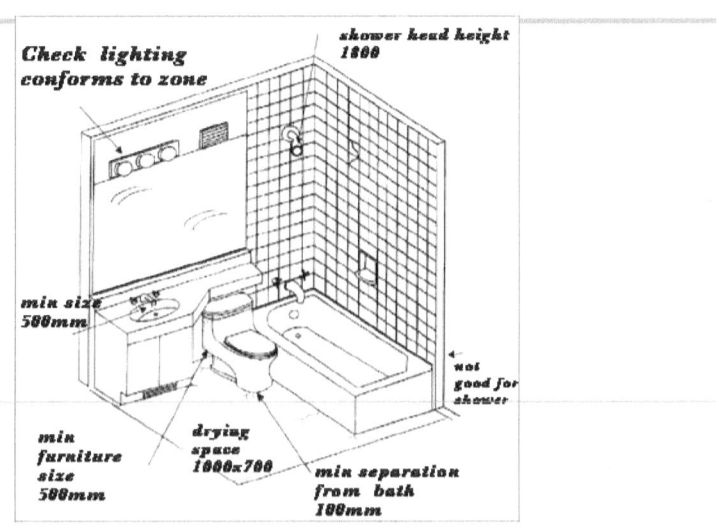

Check lighting conforms to zone

shower head height 1800

min size 500mm

min furniture size 500mm

drying space 1000x700

min separation from bath 100mm

not good for shower

Planning Guidelines

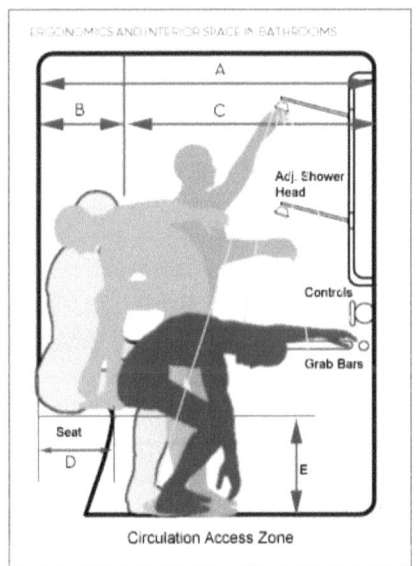

ERGONOMICS AND INTERIOR SPACE IN BATHROOMS

A

B

C

Adj. Shower Head

Controls

Grab Bars

Seat

D

E

Circulation Access Zone

A.min depth 800mm

B.additional space for seat 400-500mm

C.optimum size 1000mm

min seat depth 400mm

E.seat height 400-500mm

grab bars set at 800-1000 high

fixed shower height 1800mm slider at

1500mm valve at 1200mm

Basins

·traditional basins have an upstand
·modern basins tend to be smaller
·basins can var from45cm wide to over a metre
·many basins have a poorly designed soap ledge
·his and hers basins are ideal if space allows
·beware the old built in acrylic basins
·semi pedestal is a good option but the wall needs to be battened
·furniture options are increasingly popular

The type of basin will be dictated by the style of the bathroom. Basin sizes tend to be more restrictive with traditional style bathrooms so this may be a limiting factor.. Some of the traditional circular pedestals can be difficult to install and will probably need a flow through trap.. Pop up wastes are popular but rarely adjusted or installed properly. Remember your taps may be one tap hole - the most popular - two tap hole - the old fashioned choice or three tap hole - the classic choice. Very few basins are available as 3 tap hole but it is possible to have them drilled - you will need a friendly monumental mason but they will warn you that the drilling is purely at your own risk. Many basins are semi punched so you can select your options at the site. Please note that few plumbers are capable or will take a chance at punching through the holes in a semi punched basin. It is a quite easy task but you need a center punch, a ball pane hammer and a steady nerve and eye. Cloak basins can be as small as 200mm.

W.C.

- there is virtually no S trap just a pan connector
- you cannot legally install other than a 6/3 litre flush wc.
- almost all w.c. are now push button flush
- replacement cisterns are now a problem
- w.c.'s are more or less standard but not all dimensions are identical
- electronic flush is the future

The style of suite chosen by the customer will normally dictate the actual w.c. you will be working with. Most modern w.c. are quite compact and therefore quite easy to work with. Moving the w.c. from it's existing position is not that easy. In first floor bathrooms you will nearly always be working with the SVP which is usually in the corner of the room and you can clearly see how the w.c. is positioned in relation to the svp. Moving the w.c. closer to the svp is quite straightforward. Moving from from the svp along the same wall is also quite easy or possibly the adjacent wall. As a general rule you are best to keep the w.c. as short as possible to the stack but moving to the adjacent wall should not be a problem.

The quality of the w.c. should be an issue but rarely are they chosen for this reason. Generally speaking you will need to look at the German ranges to get some hi tech non stick finishes - very desirable.

The efficiency of the w.c.'s varies quite dramatically and the quality of the casting equally so. Some of the Chinese castings are dreadful and result in leaks from casting faults. Always try to choose a recognisable brand which will have been quality controlled to avoid these problems The biggest aggravation the bathroom supplier faces is the failure of an appliance and the w.c. is clearly the most important appliance.

Because of the water saving features of modern w.c. they are not always as good as they should be. The new 3/6 litre flush makes them compact but the reduced level flush means that they are not always as good as they should be in clearing solids or paper. Unfortunately there is no real answer you cannot magically go back to a 12 litre flush - i tis illegal to use other than the modern standard unless you are dealing with a replacement w.c. What it does mean, however, is that the w.c. is now a fairly compact device and even btw installation are used with a compact flush cistern - usually push button. Again the secret is to get the best available in the style chosen by the customer and budget allows. Spend the money on quality first and only spend on gimmicks after that choice.

Remember,, the customer does not always understand quality in the sanitary ware market and will generally be grateful for your guidance in this matter. Better quality means better performance means greater customer satisfaction.

Solid fixings are also important in these matters so the fitter needs to follow the better living guidelines as to installation techniques.

The toilet seat is also an important choice. Check the quality yourself. if you have a design related seat and therefore no choice, make absolutely sure the look and feel of the seat is what the customer would appreciate. If you choose a designer w.c. that will take just the one seat. Does it feel solid? is it hygienically designed. Does it have soft close hinges? Is it an easy clean seat i.e does it have snap on hinges so you can remove in seconds and thoroughly clean. This could very well become a bylaw requirement tin future years. Health, safety and hygiene are huge issues in the market place. A pretty place to park your bum is not necessarily the best way to choose a bathroom.

The following pages shows a selection of different w.c. types and styles. The BTW and Wall Hung w.c. are becoming increasingly popular. close coupled BTW versions are very desirable but not always easy to fit unless you have an S trap in the floor or can convert one.

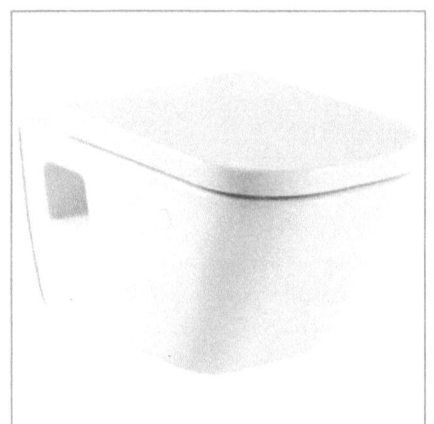

BIDET

Bidets are produced to match most w.c. suites but not all. The sales of Bidets in the U.K. are less than half that of the continent and probably less than a third of those in France - probably the home of the bidet.

Bidets are produced to match most w.c. suites but not all. The sales of Bidets in the U.K. are less than half that of the continent and probably less than a third of those in France - probably the home of the bidet. Because of this relative apathy of UK consumers you will also find that supplies of bidet's are often difficult so make sure you can access the bidet to match the style of w.c. you have chosen. If not offer something different before the customer gets set on your first choice. Availability of bathroom goods can be quite troublesome on a regular basis so you need to be in touch especially with the more demanding projects. As stated in the previous section rising spray bidets are virtually a thing of the past as the latest regulations about backflow protection make it virtually impossible to fit

The under seat or flexible bidet devices also provide a problem in this respect so care must be taken when installing any of these devices. Over the rim bidets which are the majority of those available are not a problem and can be freely specified.

See here a diagram illustrating the problem

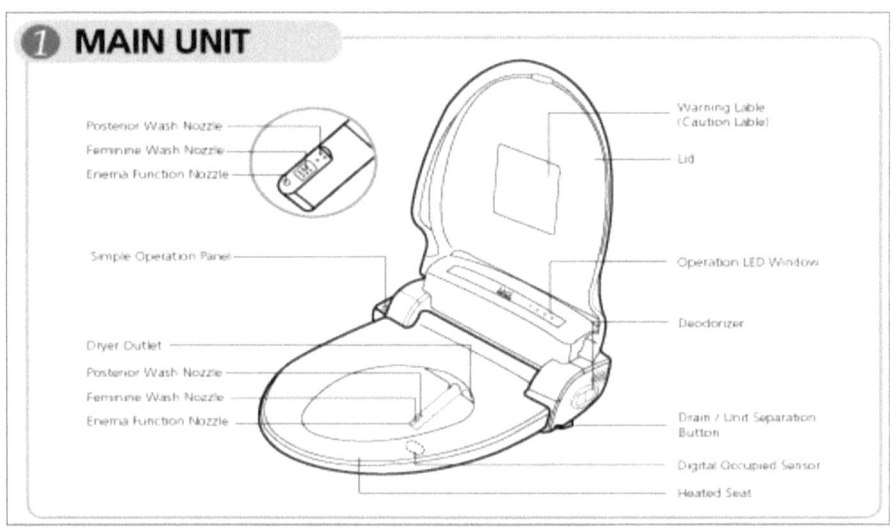

① MAIN UNIT

Posterior Wash Nozzle
Feminine Wash Nozzle
Enema Function Nozzle

Simple Operation Panel

Dryer Outlet
Posterior Wash Nozzle
Feminine Wash Nozzle
Enema Function Nozzle

Warning Lable
(Caution Lable)

Lid

Operation LED Window

Deodorizer

Drain / Unit Separation
Button

Digital Occupied Sensor

Heated Seat

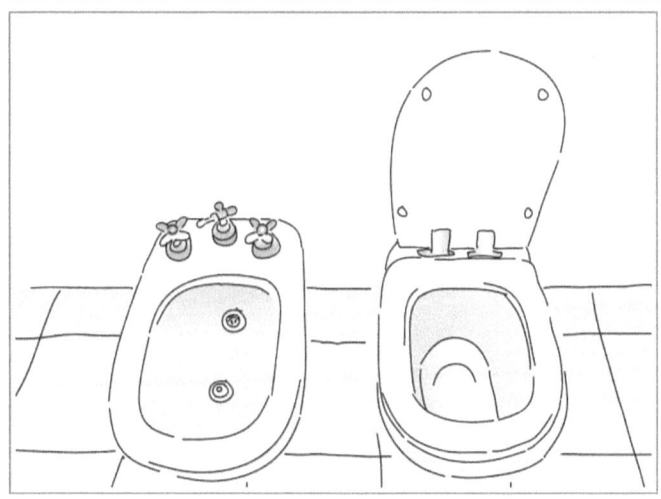

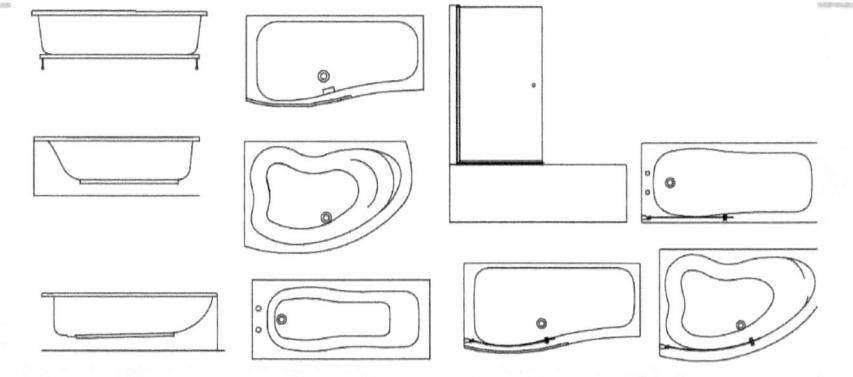

BATHS

- major point - does it fit
- does it serve your purpose
- if showering over is it suitable
- does i t suit the room style
- if buying designer taps are tap holes drilled?
- will it stand the weight subjected?
- is it a full acrylic or better surface
- do you really want a cold slippery metal bath?

Baths are made in a whole variety of substances and finishes and even colours to a certain extent. A lot of baths are simply designer items so we will not really consider these as the buyer pays his money and takes the choice and if you can really afford a designer bath you don't really need to query the choice as you will be able to afford a replacement when you tire of it or when it starts to look shabby. Even a £5k bath could look shabby very quickly and the cheap Chinese spa baths costing £1-2K might only survive a year or two.

It pays to think very carefully about your choice. if you want a roll top bath always go for a double skinned genuine acrylic bath. The surface on these quarry stone type baths can be very difficult to maintain. Solid surface is wonderful for worktops but not so great for baths and can be quite limited strength wise.

At the end of the day a bath can be a - see it and love it - choice. Hopefully having made the choice the buyer will continue to love it?

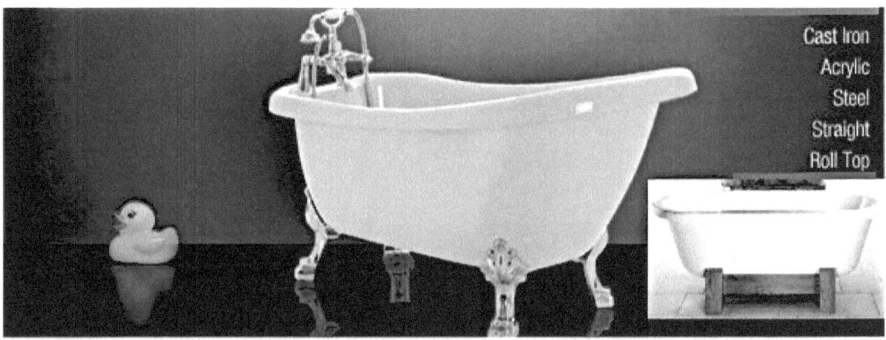

Cast Iron
Acrylic
Steel
Straight
Roll Top

We tend to glibly call this category - Roll Tops; but in reality we fit in most designs of freestanding baths whether modern or traditional

Roll top baths made a big come back some years ago with the new double acrylic baths. Resin style baths were quite a big contender for a while but the surface i is not so durable as acrylic and most buyers are probably dissatisfied with these especially after being in use for a while. There are a variety of styles in roll tops such as slipper, double slipper, single ended, double ended and a host of variations based on these themes including modern styles. Most freestanding baths started off as a roll top variant but now there are a number of, partcularly modern designs. You need a lot of space for a freestanding bath and you need to think carefully about the plumbing which can be a nightmare. If in any doubt ask your plumber to have a look before you set about installing it. Can easily turn out to be an expensive folly. Freestanding spa baths are an even bigger installation nightmare- beware.

Also please note the problem with the confusion between shrouds and standpipes Standpipes are much more expensive and allow the taps to be self suspended. Shrouds are simply to cover the pipework to the taps which are set within the tap ledge of the bath. Also check the floor for stability - even an acrylic roll to can be quite heavy when filled with water and an 18 stone bather. that is a lot of weight on the ball of a cast iron foot.

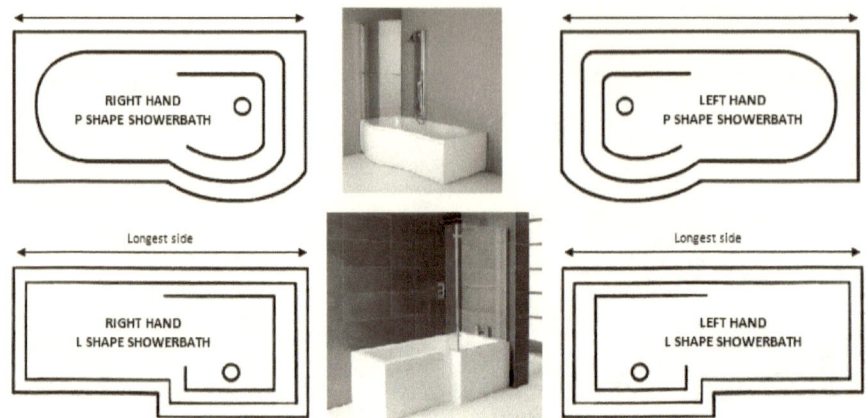

SHOWERBATHS

- standard size 1700/1500
- extra large 1800
- standard acrylic
- heavy duty like carronite
- full overbath enclosures
- traditional shower screens
- p shape or geometric

In the early days a shower bath was an ordinary bath with a screen or enclosure. These are still available but conventional baths are not generally designed for showering over. where space permits the P shape bath or the new geometric shape shower bath is easily the best choice. Although they are a little wider at the showering end than a conventional bath you should be able to find this space quite easily even in an conventional British bathroom. As they are mostly acrylic there is a flat non slip area for showing. Couple this with a good placement of grips (not on the bath) then you have what might be considered the perfect package. It is certainly the most practical package If you decide to remove your bath and install only a shower you make the house less salable - a point to remember.

Apart from the fact that all showerbaths are left or right handed and varying sizes there is little else to consider for planning purposes except for the plumbing. However a little point to note when you are conducting a survey - check out the possibility of a stair wedge. Quite often especially in the smaller houses the bathroom is built over the stair wedge and the bath sloping end is built over the stair wedge so when you take out the bath there is a wedge shape lump at the sloping end. You would find it difficult if not impossible to install a shower bath in this kind of layout - check carefully.

Although shower baths have taken a fair share of the market and a great number of people change completely to showering which is clearly a more hygienic choice there are still a lot of standard baths installed today. One point I think it is worth making and has been made especially to the hotel trade is the use of cheap metal baths. The hotel trade understandably selected a lot of these cheap nasty baths as you can pick up a quantity of steel baths for £20 or less and they do feel solid. But the enamel finish makes them very vulnerable and easy to chip but the glass finish more importantly makes them quite lethal to shower over. If you have ever stood up in a steel bath you will understand. the slightest movement and you are over or out of the bath. I have had many spills in cheap steel baths with slipper bases especially in soft or softer water. Indeed at one point I nearly sued the now defunct Premier Travel Inn group but I didn't have time. The even more criminal lack of care is displayed and still displayed by not placing any grab rails on the wall or sometimes even anywhere. DISGUSTING.

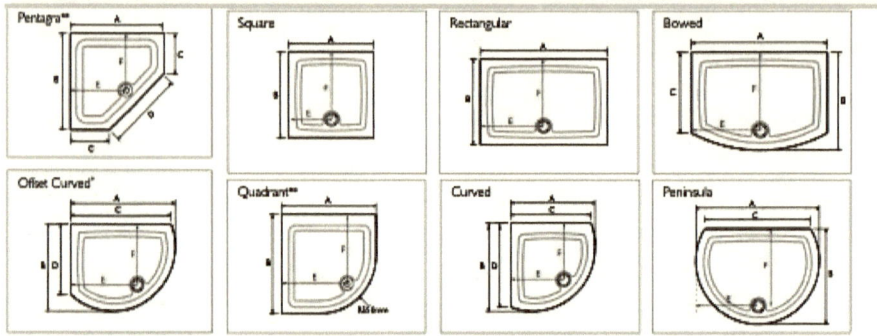

Showering

- quadrant - various sizes and handing
- square and rectangular with or without side panels
- trays in different sizes and thicknesses and materials including the latest designer slim line styles
- walk in showers - with proper trays or for use in wet rooms - if the property and installation permits - you need to be very careful with this one
- make sure the quality of the shower suits the showering facility you want - power showers need better enclosures

Gone are the days when a planner would specify a cheap plastic enclosure or one of the old fashioned ideal Standard steel cubicles. Today the choice of showers is a common decision, virtually all executive houses have a separate shower room and many of these 1960's house designs have had their enclosures changed two or three times If they had installed a decent shower and tray in the first instance there would have been no need.

You can also buy steam cabins and products but this is an entirely different choice and a more niche market so we have left this as a separate subject further on in the book.

Many buyers now insist on both a shower and a bath in their only bathroom or even in their master bathroom. The medical profession is unanimous in their recommendation of showers. especially where bathrooms are shared by a number of people. Clearly no one wants to bathe in their own or anyone else's filth. Showers have been the biggest growth area in the bathroom market for many, many years. It is probably the most important topic in the majority of bathrooms so study the options carefully.

Your first decision is whether or not to use a shower tray and which style and type to select.

Wet rooms have become a fad but the reality is they are not a great choice for British bathrooms. You will see many successful wet rooms on the continent or in hotels and they are built usually on concrete floors. In the UK with the wooden fabrication of the building, if there is a flaw in the 'tanking' of the wet room, water will inevitably seep out and over a period of years damage the structure of the building. Could be a very expensive error. Use only a very experienced installer or don't do it. Shower trays are now available in 25mm height - you could even flush this with the rest of the floor to achieve a perfect wet room look without the hassle.

When it comes to the choice of shower tray material unfortunately we have a problem in the UK whereby stone resin trays have been given an undeserved reputation. In fact stone resin trays are very solid but have only a gel coat surface which is frankly, rubbish. What is the most efficient tray is an acrylic tray with it's wonderful durable surface but with a resin backing. Usually found in slimline trays no more than about 50mm thick these are installer friendly and guaranteed for some considerable time, usually a minimum of 10 years. Choose wisely but do not choose an old fashioned fibreglass tray - these are bigger rubbish than stone resin

Fur-
niture has been a feature of British bathrooms for many years. Indeed the first furniture I was selling was way back in the late 60's when Metlex introduced their revolutionary bathroom modules including modular w.c.'s and bidets which fully blended into the furniture group. Unfortunately it was some years before its time and certainly was not a seller from our viewpoint.

FURNITURE
- modular furniture
- vanity units
- fully fitted furniture bathrooms
- exotic vanity units
- matching wall units
- matching mirrors

Furniture today tends to be concentrated on modular unis rather than fitted bathrooms. There are many of these on the market mostly in high gloss white and generally speaking of European manufacture but the Chinese and beginning to offer more in this market sector.

The Chinese already dominate the exotic market of very stylish vanity units with side cabinets, mirrors etc. In a variety of wood and laminate finishes they are reasonably priced and reasonable quality.

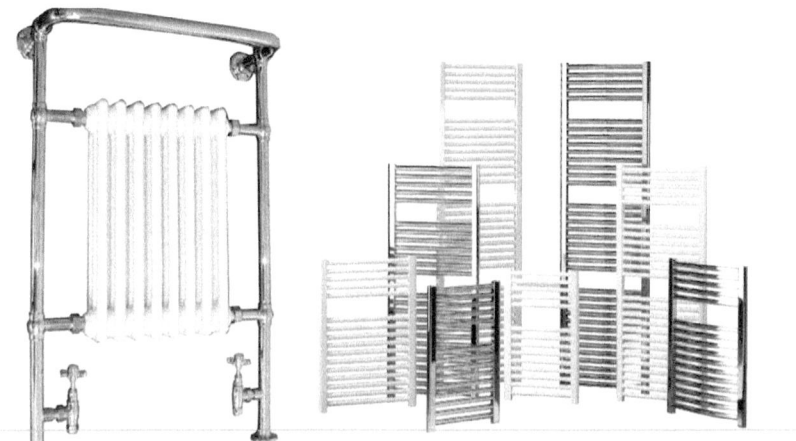

TOWEL RAILS
RADIATORS

·for simplicity choose electric
·watch for direct and indirect use
·is it made from mild steel
·is it made from brass
·is it made from copper
·non corrosive is best
·is it meant to heat the room
·what is the heat output

Towel rails and towel radiators are a popular item to finish the bathroom. However you need to check the size of the rad and the ambient temperature of the house. A modern centrally heated house will probably not need anything too large in output but an old draughty Victorian building might need a full heating solution. The Victorian style towel radiators are some of the highest output models available but beware most of these have steel radiator sections which are not suitable for direct systems. Check the with manufacturer who will usually advise which is suitable. If it is stainless steel or chrome or copper or brass that is ok but steel is usually forbidden for direct systems. If you cannot find the central heating plumbing you can buy electric rads or you can convert almost any of them to electric. If you are spending a few quid on a rad please remember the decorative valves - shame to spoil the job.

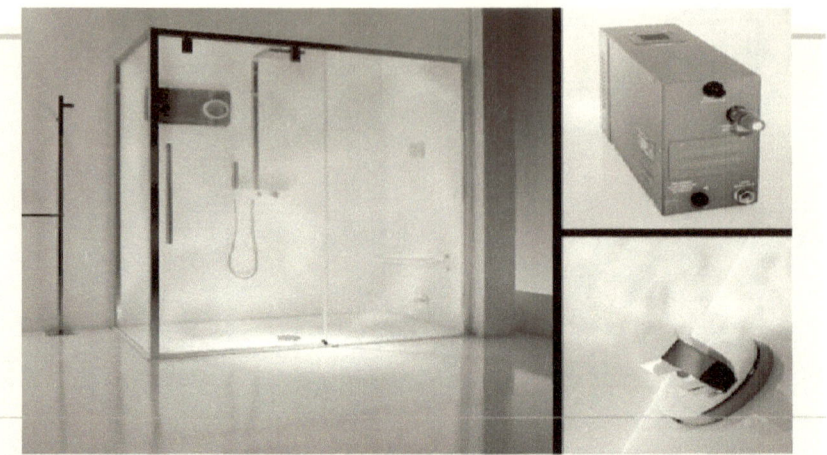

STEAM - SAUNA

·is the room naturally ventilated
·is that enough
·if no windows a fan is
mandatory
·is the fan ductable or window
fitted
·if ductable how?
·is this a steam proof
environment or will ventilation
be required because of
paintwork
·are you installing steam =
ventilation is essential

The question of steam is quite important as in many respects this is far more valuable than a whirlpool bath for example. Although the sales of steam do not quite reach
those of spa systems there is still a significant market. and,
of course, the value of the bathroom is signifcant so well
worth the effort to get the sale and do an efficient job.

There are a number of ways you can approach steam. You
can buy an all in one stem enclosure or a steam bath or pre-
pare your own enclosure and install a steam generator. This
is the best way by far and the life expectancy of a steam installation could be as long as 20 years - the life of a steam
package , especially the cheap Chinese products, could be
as little as 2 years. Don't confuse a steam shower with a
sauna they are quite different but it is possible to combine
the two in one package.

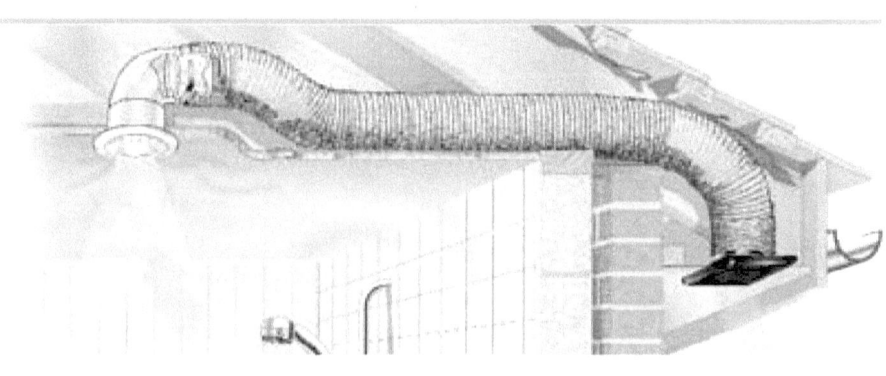

VENTILATION

- if you have no windows it is the law
- keeps smells at bay
- even if you have a window do you want it open in the winter?
- steam showers must be ventilated
- helps control mold
- keeps bathroom decor fresh and clean and slows

It has always surprised me that so many people build a lovely new bathroom costing £1000's and don't protect their investment by ventilating the room. Bathrooms are damp anyway and showers are damper still. Control this with a proper adequate sized fan. A variable contol with a humidistat would be the best choice but any fan is better than nothing. Best to have one that is controllable rather than just comes on with the light. Often people forget to turn these things off and burn out the motor. Also purchasing a quality product means longer lasting and lower noise levels. Choose and buy wisely. You will find most fans clearly marked with their capability.

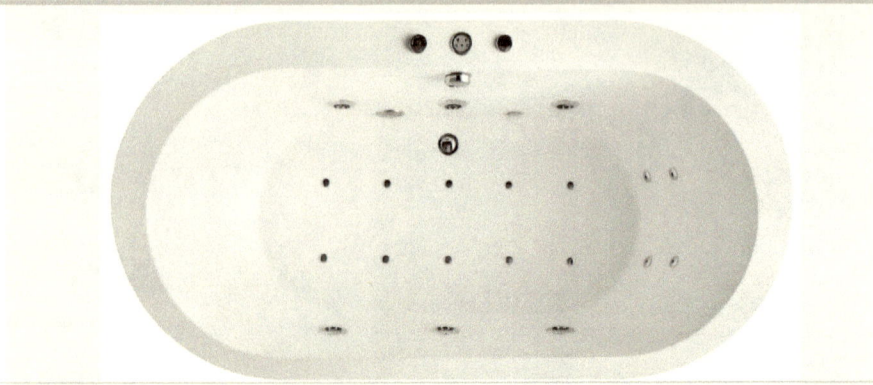

TYPES OF WHIRLPOOLS

* *Standard jets*
* *jacuzzi style jets*
* *micro jets*
* *standard aspiration*
* *turbo - blown aspiration*
* *pneumatic controls*
* *electronic controls*

A whirlpool is a spa bath that pumps water through a variety of jets from about 100mm down to about 50mm. Air is normally induced by a vortex to give a bubbly effect but it is the power of the water that provides the real massage effect. The air effect can be enhanced by linked an air blower to the system to provide powered air through the system and a much enhanced effect.

Clearly, as with any bath, there must be dirt from the bathers and this will accumulate in the system. this can also include fatty substances.

THIS MUST BE CLEANED AS A MATTER OF ROUTINE AND MUST BE AT LEAST MONTHLY IF BY ONE FAMILY USE OR EACH TIME IF MIXED USE

The airspa has long been promoted as a health product. In fact it has very little therapeutic effect compared to a whirlpool but in very large baths such as the maharajah style baths which can measure 2 metres by 1.5 metes an airspa is quite important to fill the hole that will be in the middle of the whirlpool bath. \Whirlpool jets only extend about

400mm into the bath and as the jets are at the sides of the bath only the airspa jets can fill that void

The airspa system or at least the blower also provides a welcome boost to the bubbly effect in a whirlpool bath which is otherwise just a passive system using a vortex.

We have found over the years that lighting in the whirlpool or airspa bath add s a really stunning extra at a very modest cost. In some cases it would be as little as £50 or so using very simple switching.

The big growth area came with led lighting which is far superior to the old system that required lamp changes which can be very fiddly

the LED lamps can come in various colours or clear and now quite inexpensive colour changing lights

Colour changing is not the same as chromatherapy and thi sis the area that alternative medicine advocates will recommend to you. Well worth offering

This is just another kind of whirlpool bath following the American glitz method of piling in the features including in line heaters. Unfortunately in line heaters are one of the most unreliable aspect of any whirlpool bath and if the heater fails you are un-

likely to be able to obtain a spare part, although you could cuy in a standard heater but as pipe sizes are not universal this often needs to be a bodge up. These baths are often made in very small factories in China with no sense of standardisation and no real production of spare parts. If you want a short term purchase with lots of gadgets this may be for you but otherwise stick to a standard production whirlpool using normal replacable parts from European SUPPLIERS.

At the start of our whirlpool success we started to sell a lot of good quality whirlpool kits. These were mainly from French manufacturers and used standard sized pipework and were fairly simple to construct although not strictly a DIY project.

However they were very reliable and very popular. There were and are a lot of cheap flexible hose kits about and latterly the really cheap Chinese kits.

I recall one of our suppliers talking abou the recent demo of a Chinese kit as he watched and saw the pump overheat and catch fire - not inspiring.

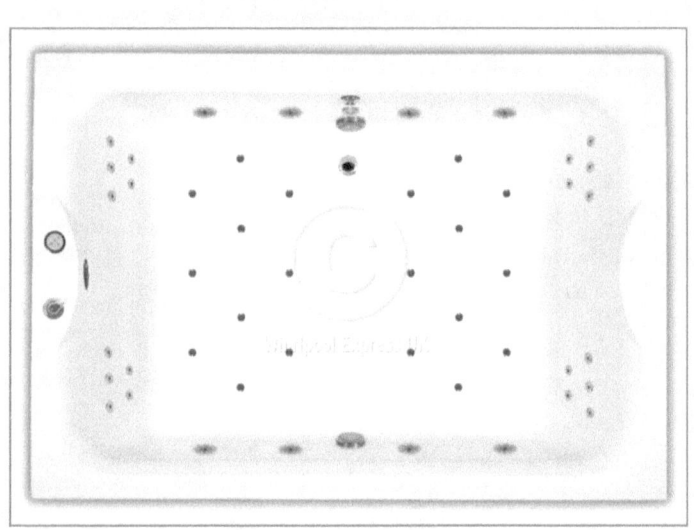

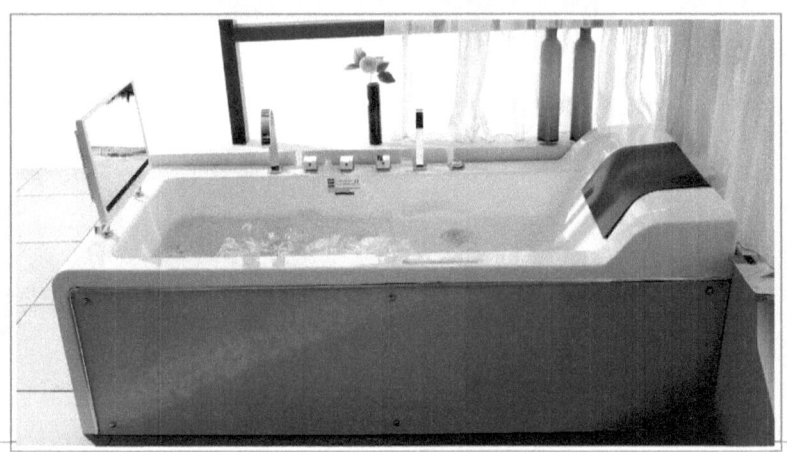

Brassware

BRASSWARE
SHOWER FITTINGS
·bar valve as above- simple and effective
·concealed valve - stylish
·concealed triple valve for body jets
·grand riser for the best of both
·shower tower for glitzy showering but short life
·hydromassage panels or cubicle for all in one convenience but short life
·maybe look at steam
·a back up electric shower but not for main use

This is the most complex decision that will have to be made in any bathroom or shower room. Even in a bathroom with just a bath, most buyers will no longer be satisfied with a bath only facility. Over 90% of buyers will want a showering facility even if it is just over the bath. so the decision is as per the list on the left except that you might want a combined bath filler and shower fitting perhaps even a bath shower mixer which you can purchase in bar valve format as well although cost will be as much a factor as style. A bath/shower facility could cost from maybe as little as £100 or it could run into £1000's. clearly , many cases you will have to consider a pump. A gravity shower is really a waste of time. The head of water in most gravity shower rooms will be tiny and not fit for purpose. Combi boilers solve a lot of those problems and most people are quite satisfied with that facility. By itself it probably is not adequate for body jets but a combi boiler with a slave cylinder will do the job. There is no escaping the fact that an unvented cylinder with a full 3 bar pressure and a good water flow will always be the best choice as long as the site is suitable. In most urban situations this is ok but rural installations may be a problem.

FINAL DECOR

POINTS TO NOTE

❖ *what is the theme is the decor true to the theme*

❖ *is the customer staying in the property - how long*

❖ *don't make the final decor too outrageous or overly personal they may want to sell the scheme in the future*

❖ *is the decor in keeping with the rest of the property - does it complement the property or detract from it*

The final decor obviously depends upon the style of bath-room chosen together with the buyer and what the buyer's personal taste dictates. It is always worth pointing out, however, that if the design is tooo outlandish and the cus-tomer wishes to move at some time in the future you need to choose a theme which can be sold to a third part.

WHAT TYPE OF LIGHTING?

* *we have already discussed whirlpool lighting - very highly recommended*
* *similarly steam shower lighting*
* *but lighting in an ordinary shower is very desirable similar styles to steam*
* *chromatherapy is used for spa and steam*
* *whatever lighting is chosen remember baths are hot and steamy - make sure they are easy to keep clean*
* *you must note the allowable electrics in the various zones*

It never ceases to amaze me how varied the taste in lighting appears to be. Although the traditional look is quite keen in bathrooms still there should be no reason why you would have frilly types of fittings and shades that would be almost impossible to keep clean. It is also essential to have lighting over the basin, shaving station and make up area which may be one and the same and can often be incorporated in the mirror - pLenty of choice.

And remember all lighting should be modern energy saving and notably the new led ranges -

LED IS KING

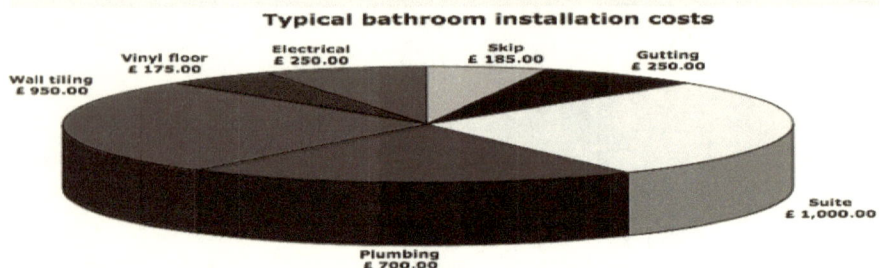

Typical bathroom installation costs

Vinyl floor £ 175.00 · Wall tiling £ 950.00 · Electrical £ 250.00 · Skip £ 185.00 · Gutting £ 250.00 · Suite £ 1,000.00 · Plumbing £ 700.00

INSTALLATION

The tendency for homeowners to undertake their own installation for a project as large as a bathroom is now diminishing. Entrusting £1000's to an amateur is obviously questionable and the time it would take for an amateur to complete such a large project would drive his/her spouse to distraction. When you are younger you probably think that you can accomplish this massive feat, when you get older you tend to be more realistic and want to ensure tht the end product is of a high standard. there are also many regulation which prevent an unqualified person undertaking these jobs and the insurance implications are huge- not worth the risk.

The average DIYer is competent for simple jobs but when you encounter the new speedfit plumbing it is easy to get caught lacking and when it comes to the large soil pipe for the w.c., Bad News - leave it to the professionals and save yourself a lot of grief. It isn't cheap but if you get stuck it will cost even more to rectify. And you probably don't have the best tools such as pipe bending equipment which can save quite a bit on fittings. Your plumber will have these

Electrics are critical in a bathroom. You should by now have covered the section on bathroom zones for electrics and i rating of lighting in the zones within a bathroom. clearly you will also have other electrics in the bathroom such as a whirlpool or other spa bath which requires special consideration. For example a novice electrician as most plumbers are, will probably want to install an ELCB for the whirlpool bath and yet if you already have one on the existing system another one could become a problem rather than a benefit. also remember that some bathrooms may have high unit items such as a Steam Generator or an Electric Shower. These items could take 30 amps of more. In fact some steam generators need 3 phase which the average household would not have and could not economically install.

A lot of plumbers think they are tilers. One of our last bathroom refits had a very good plumber who stepped in at the last minute as our original plumber had to be chucked out because he was useless. The replacement plumber made a very good job overall until it came to the tiling. He took almost 4 days to fit 6 sq.. yards of tiles. This was at least twice as long as it should have taken

We also used to have on our team a very coarse but very very conscientious and competent plumber/bathroom fitter/kitchen fitter. He used to both amuse us and frighten us when it came to gas fitting in the kitchen. He would lie there with his head in the sink unit working on the gas with a roll your own fag hanging out of his mouth. he was as happy as a sandboy. Luckily today this would be illegal but his real downfall was his tiling. Don't get me wrong the quality was excellent but it was so slow. he also had very little technical knowledge about tiles. He could not recognise or appreciate the tile designs. On one job he did the tiling - 20 sq. yards, while the householder was away. When the buyer returned home and admired Gordon's work he said 'it's great but all the decor tiles are upside down. He Hadn't noticed and he had to replace these expensive tiles out of his own pocket.

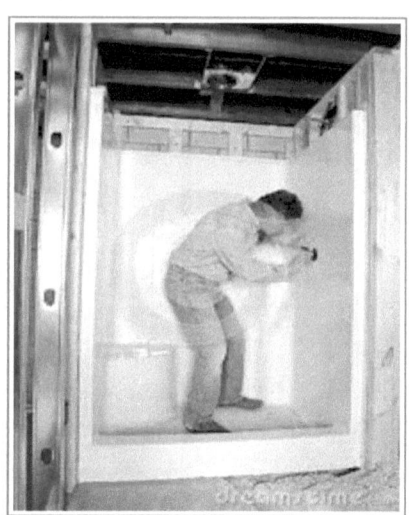

Survey

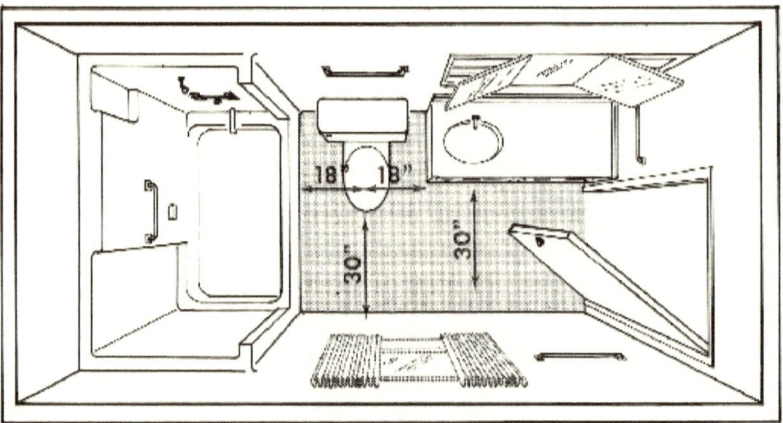

Before you can plan a bathroom you need to know the layout and measurements of the room and all the architectural features of the room. You also need to know the location of the services and you need to understand the limitations of altering these services . For further info read the kitchen guide or email support. The scale plan and axonomettric should be drawn in 1:20 scale

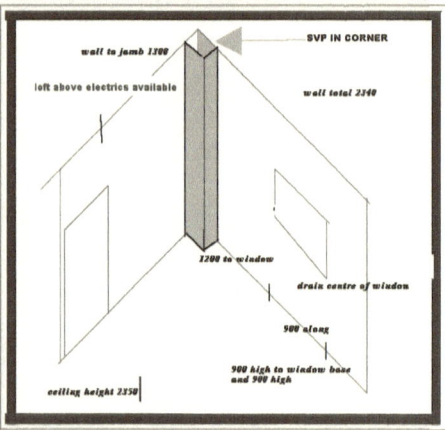

ACCESSORIES

After we have made the big sale we tend to breathe a sigh of relief and give up on the add-ons. Wrong! We should pursue those very lucrative accessories. Various small items like toilet roll holders, towel rails, toothbrush and mug and larger items such as mirrors, cabinets - especially stainless steel cabinets and all the better with some good lighting and if possible fitted with a shaver socket,

maybe a clock or maybe even a fitted TV? Could be worth £1000's

SUPPORT

Thank you for purchasing this latest version of our Bathroom Planning guide.

We want you to enjoy this publication and learn from it,

To this end we offer TOTAL SUPPORT - if you feel you need help or clarification on any points please log in to our website at

www.kbb2000.com

you will need to provide your full details and a copy of your purchase receipt and we will provide one on one assistance by email.

DISABLED BATHROOMS

We looked at ergonomics and anthropometrics and of course this applies to a bathroom as much as a kitchen. This thinking applies greatly to the w.c. which may need to be higher and to the basin which may need to have wheelchair space. the grab bars and folding rails are also specified in the DocM disabled doeument and you may wish to include more around the bath or showers. There are a number of walk in baths but they are expensive and short lived. The best option is a walk in shower possibly in the form of a wet room.

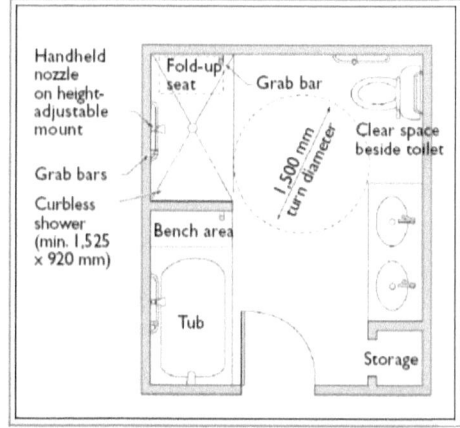

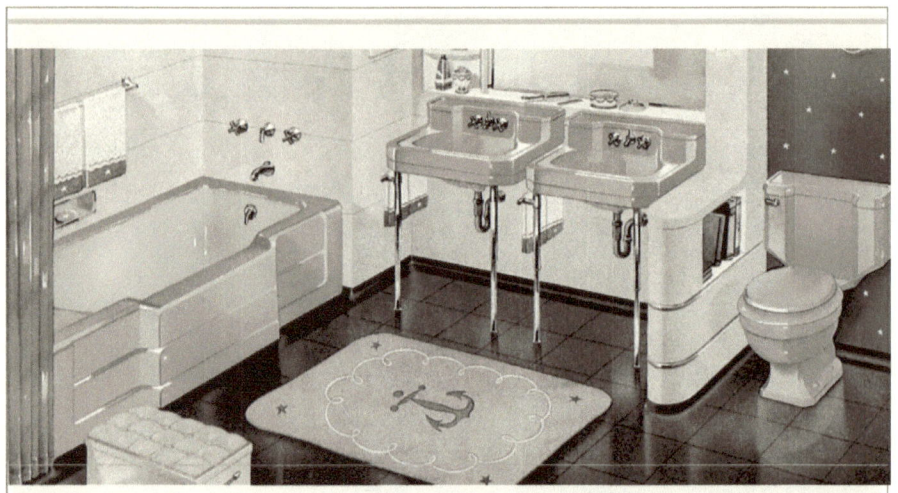

3

Bathrooms of 1950

No matter how bad you think the bathrooms of the 1960\s you need to check out these diabolical creations from the 1950< Many of them are from the good old U.S.A. And the Colours?

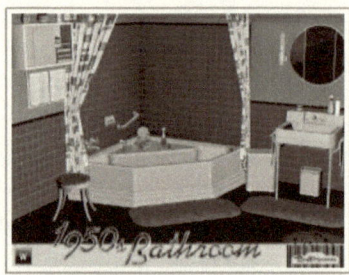

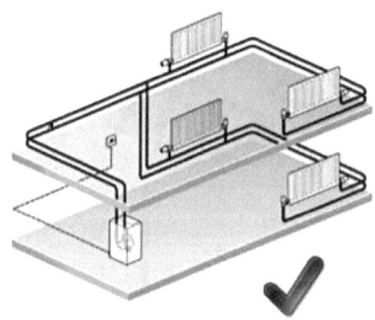

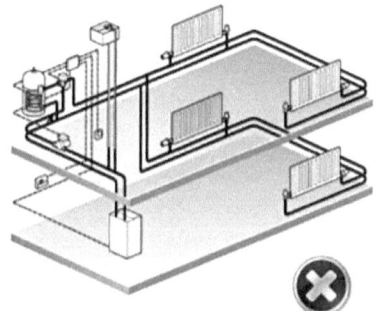

The popular combination system   Typical old-type system with cylinder, tanks etc

4

PLUMBING

Bathroom
Technical

Why do I want to know about plumbing? was the typical comment made by the delegates on the bathroom course: Our reply - BATHROOMS ARE MAINLY ABOUT PLUMBING - If you don`t understand at least the basics of plu,bing how can you plan a bathroom? On the next page you will find a typical traditional British Bathroom. There is the mains water co,ing into; usually; the kitchen with mains water feeding only the kitchen sink and area. The rest of the supply is via the storage tank in the loft: THIS IS LOW PRESSURE. Maybe 0.5 bar or less: the mains water pressure should be around 2-3 bar - 6 x that of the tank pressure: Who cares? The brassware cares - especially the shower.

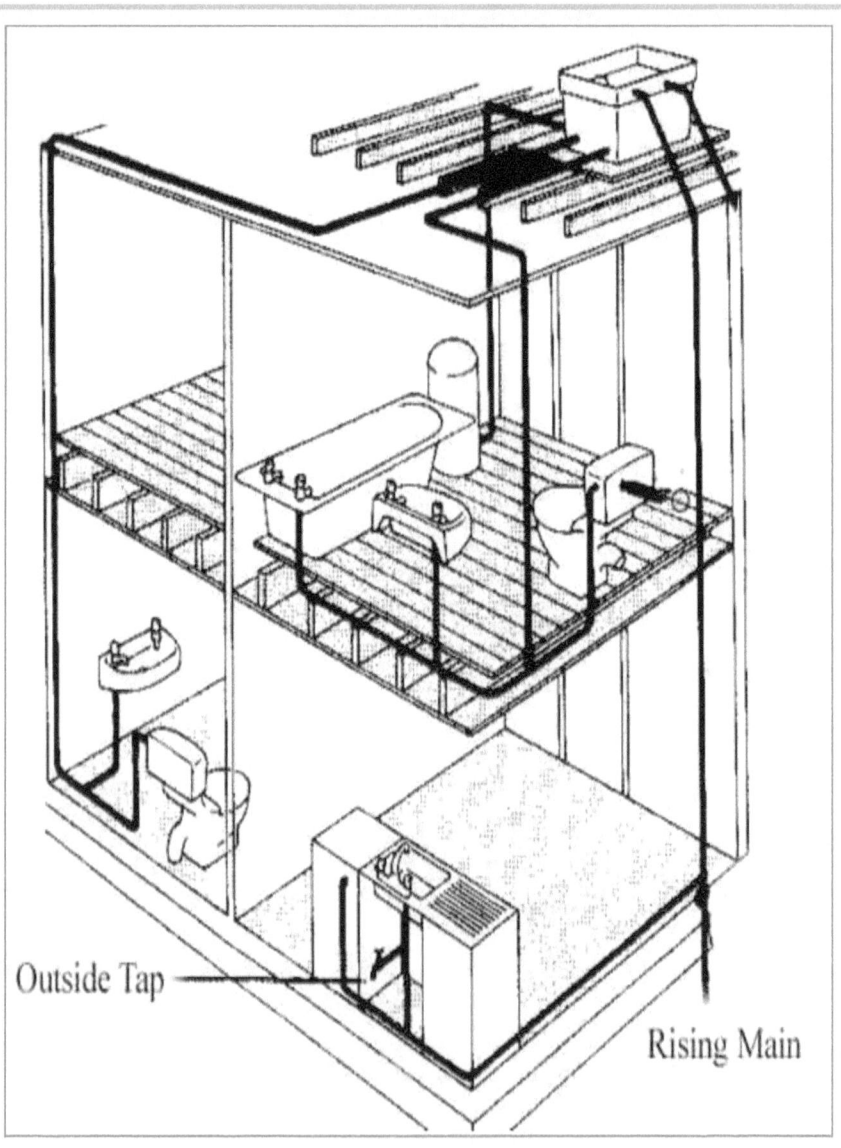

Outside Tap

Rising Main

The next examples are the unvented water system and the most popular and newest preference the combi boiler plan.

One of the recurring problems with the traditional system is the performance of the brassware. Taps used to be made to work within the limitations of the system   Some of those big old fashioned looking taps used to be able to deliver quite a good performance but the British Standard changed some years ago, so newer taps, even if they look similar, will not deliver the same amount of water. So baths take a long time to fill etc. Also the majority of brassware is now imported - from countries that only use pressurised systems so have no history of low pressure systems.

So it is quite critical to recommend the brassware suitable for the customer's system. In general terms if the brassware looks modern it will now work well on a gravity system. If it looks traditional it will probably work ok but showers really won't work at all under a gravity system.

UNVENTED HOT WATER SYSTEM

Sealed Heating System (Unvented DHW)
The optimum system for a modern installation. A pressurised hot water cylinder will provide up to 72 litres per minute of hot water at mains pressure.

This system may be marginally more expensive to install, however it is a "keep it simple" engineered solution for the supply of domestic hot water.

There are no tanks in the loft to protect from frost and the cylinder can be located at ground floor level, for example alongside the boiler.

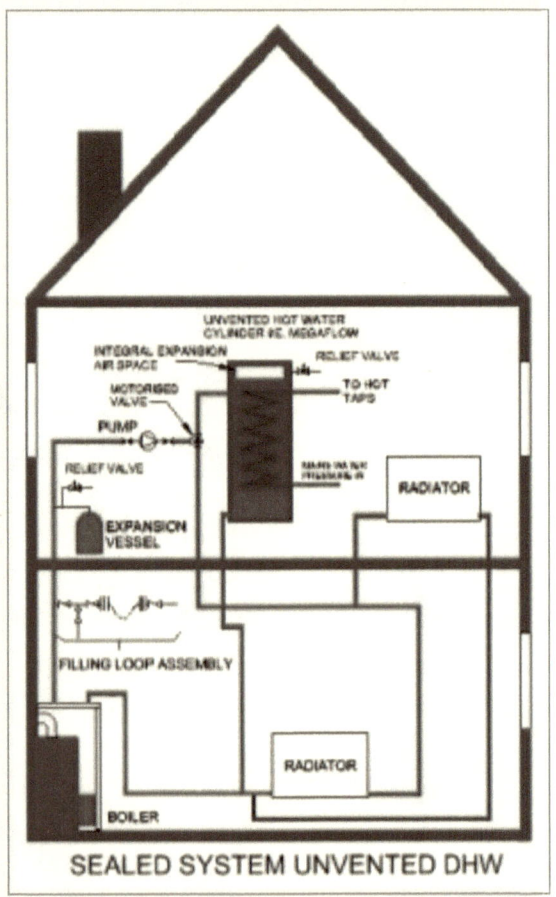

SEALED SYSTEM UNVENTED DHW

Very tidy - no tanks. Economical - hot water when needed. All water is under pressure usually about 3 bat but the flow rate is nowhere near that of an unvented system and depends upon the efficiency and size of the boiler p probably around 15 litres a minute - ok for most purposes but not for body jet showering.

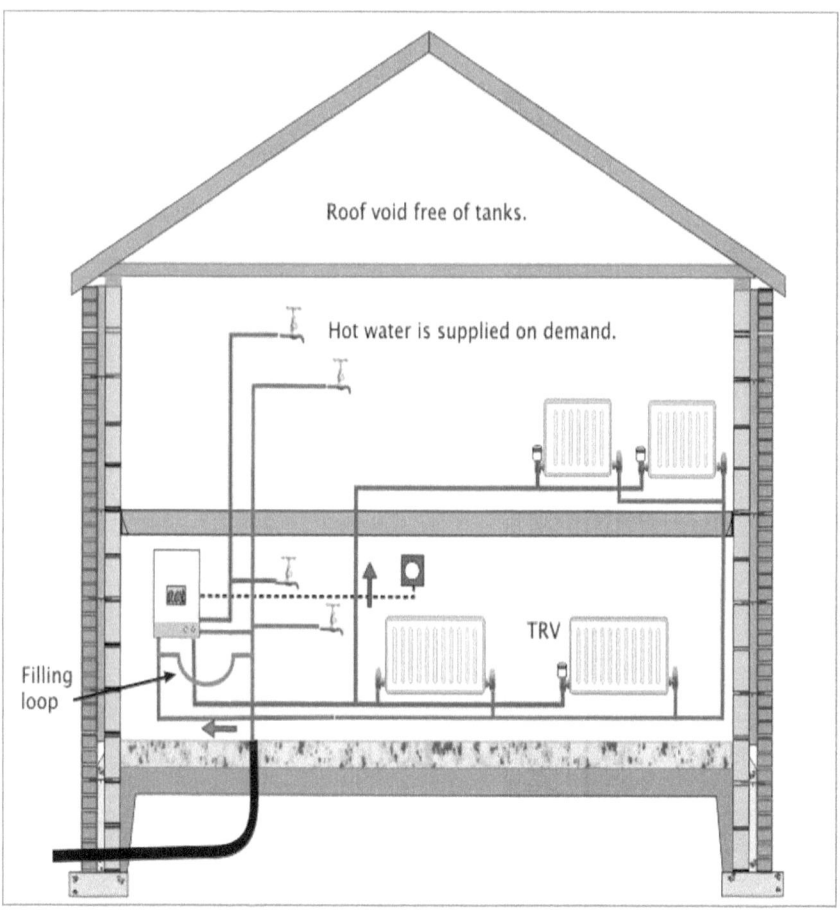

Roof void free of tanks.

Hot water is supplied on demand.

TRV

Filling loop

Bathroom technical - The Waste

OK we can now get the water into the appliances = How do we get it out - efficiently? This can be one of the bigger puzzles for the novice but in general terms it is quite simple. For any waste to work it must have a minimum drop. That means unless there is a minimum fall away from the appliance - e.g. a bath, the water will not flow away and will provide regular blockages for the customer - not a good thing to occur.

So use your common sense. Large appliances such as a bath and a toilet have the largest waste pipes and need the most efficient fall awayffrom the appliance. But it

must be within limits. Too much slope away will cause problems.

A BATH WASTE SHOULD HAVE AN AVERAGE OF 1:20 FALL

A TOILET WASTE SHOULD HAVE AN AVERAGE OF 1:40 FALL

e.g. for every unit along you (say 20) you need 1 unit down

This is the most common waste pipe system using a soil and vent pipe in plastic. All of the appliances send their waste to a branch on the vented stack. The length of that waste pipe is clearly critical according to the size of the waste and the quantity of water it must carry.

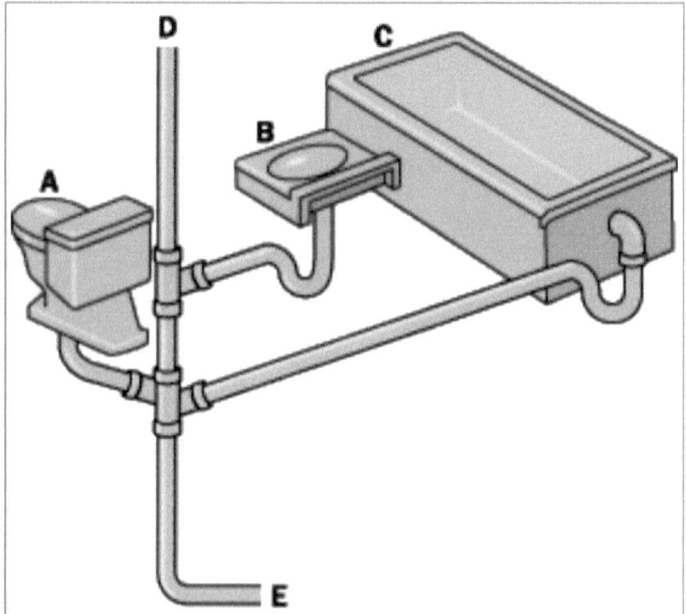

This is a dagram of a typical bathroom plumbing in a modern house. This applies to almost every house since the mid 60's. Typically you walk into the bathroom and you see that square boxing in in the corner of the room. Qll the appliance wastes go to that point. **KEEP IT SIMPLE AND SHORT**

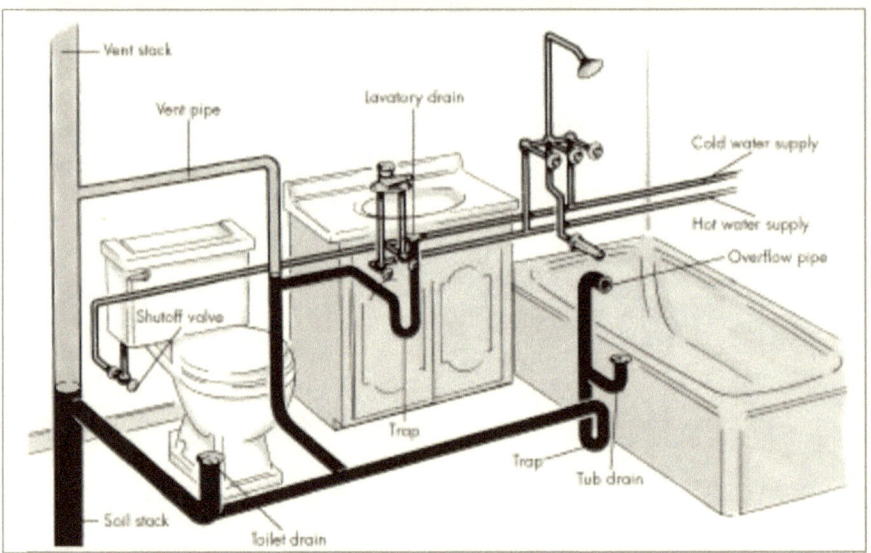

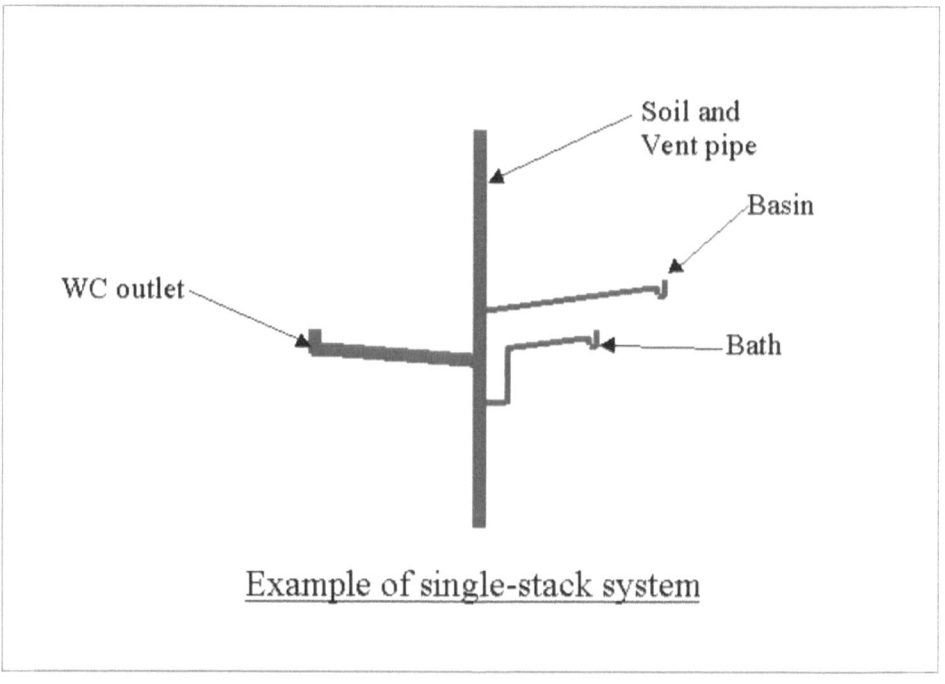

Example of single-stack system

SVP SERVES HOUSE

As you can see the svp
extends to the entire house
on all floors and possibly
even into the loft. There
may be two svp in larger
property.

Old house have a cast iron
system which is usually
fragmented but can be
converted to plastic.

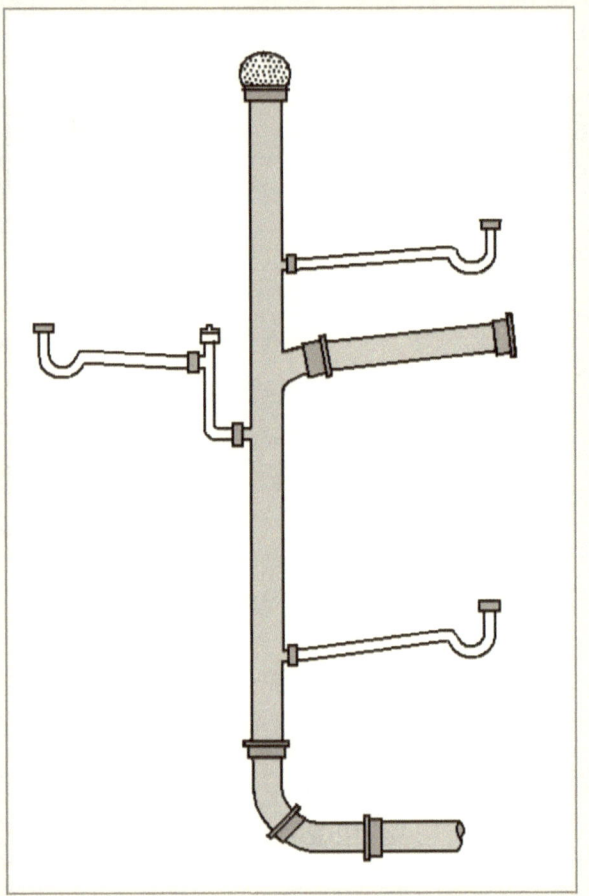

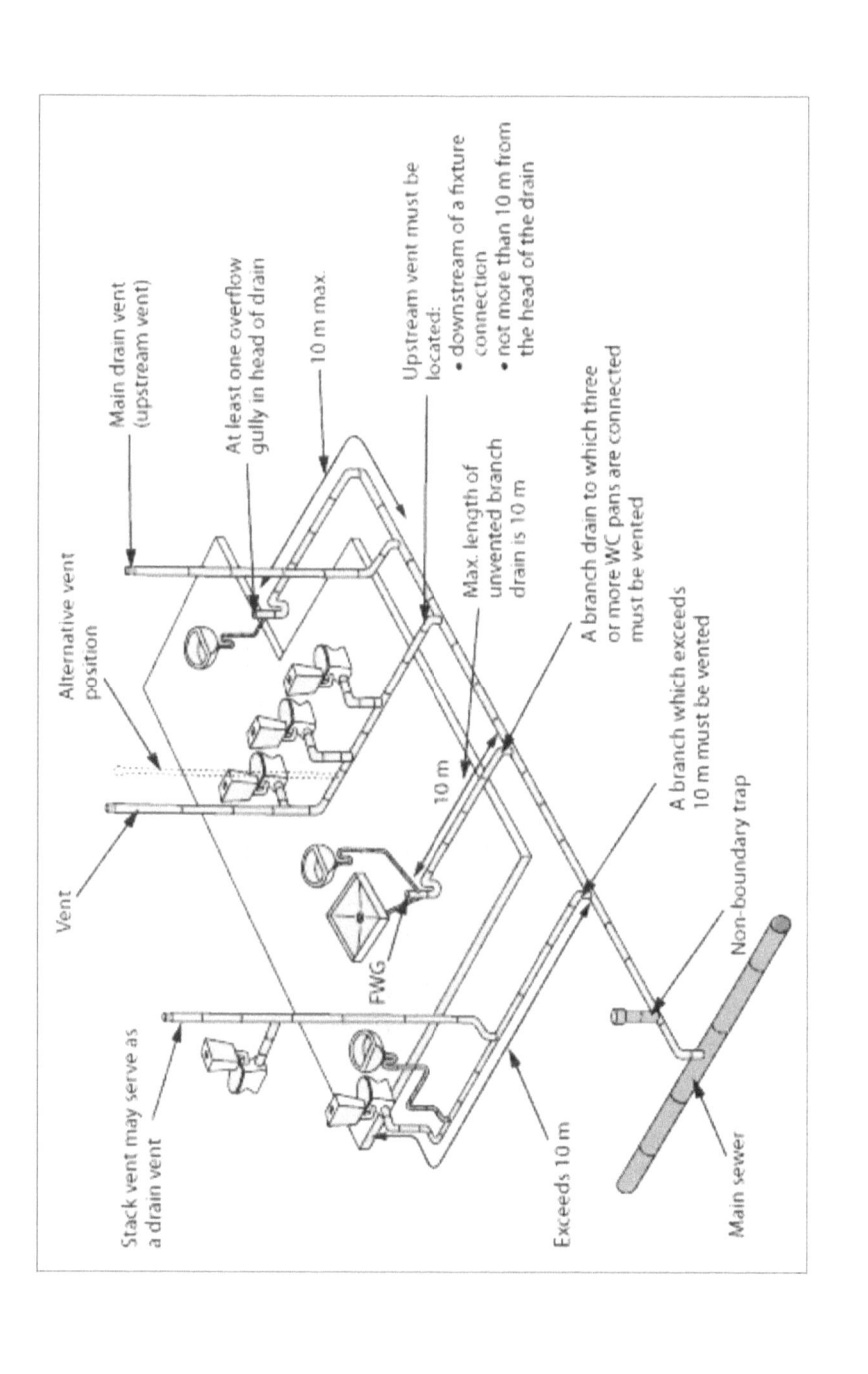

Main drain vent (upstream vent)

At least one overflow gully in head of drain

10 m max.

Upstream vent must be located:
• downstream of a fixture connection
• not more than 10 m from the head of the drain

Alternative vent position

Vent

Max. length of unvented branch drain is 10 m

A branch drain to which three or more WC pans are connected must be vented

10 m

FWG

A branch which exceeds 10 m must be vented

Stack vent may serve as a drain vent

Exceeds 10 m

Non-boundary trap

Main sewer

Don't underestimate the requirements of the shower waste. this waste could be the lowest item in the room and therefore the most difficult to provide the optimum fall. Modern showers could deliver 40 or 50 litres a minute. possibly many times more than any other waste.

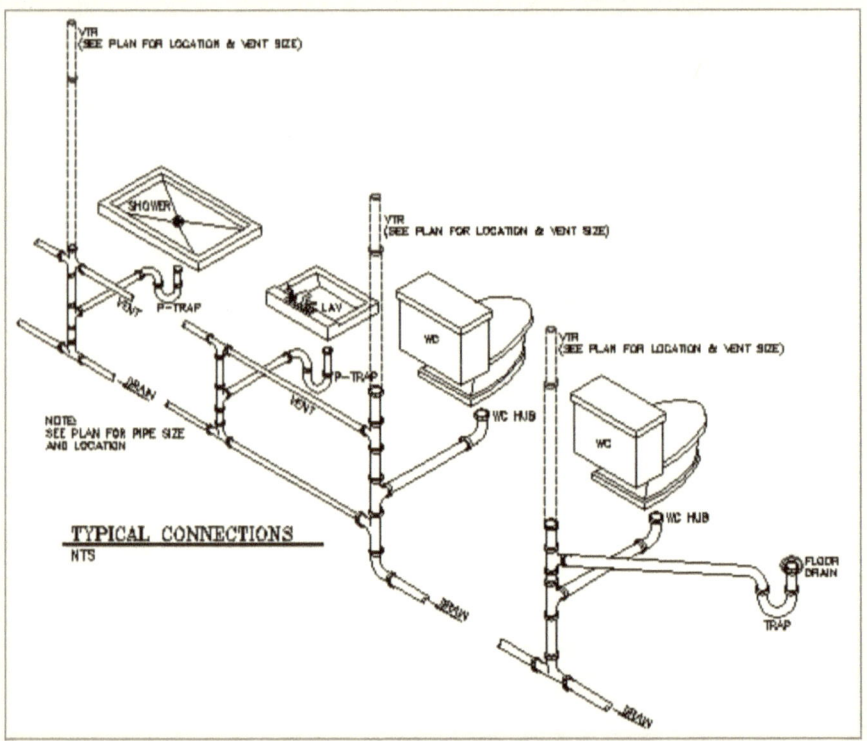

MACERATORS

Macerators can be a life saver to provide a full bathroom facility virtually anywhere in the house and even in a basement. The macerators have a set ability to pump along or pump up or a combination of both. Some are made just for the wc. and others can accept other wastes such as from a basin or shoewr. MAKE SURE YOU CHOOSE THE CORRECT VERSION - The cost varies according to capabilities. Always remember this is a pump that makes a noise. Use only if necessary and with a mind to anyone near the source of the noise.

If you believe the installation is going to be sensitive use the best quality macerator available.

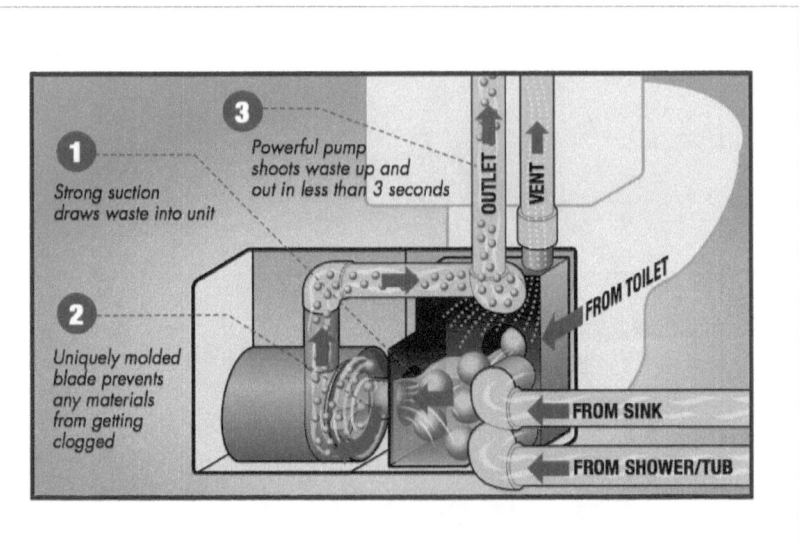

1 Strong suction draws waste into unit

2 Uniquely molded blade prevents any materials from getting clogged

3 Powerful pump shoots waste up and out in less than 3 seconds

OUTLET

VENT

FROM TOILET

FROM SINK

FROM SHOWER/TUB

	SANIFLO	SANISLIM	SANITOP	SANIPRO	SANIPACK	SANISHOWER	SANIPLUS	SANIVITE	SANICOMPACT	SANICHASSE	SANIBEST
WC	✓	✓	✓	✓	✓		✓		✓	✓	✓
WASHBASIN		✓	✓	✓	✓	✓	✓	✓	✓	✓	✓
BATH							✓				✓
SHOWER		✓		✓	✓	✓	✓				✓
POWERSHOWER*				✓			✓				✓
BIDET		✓		✓	✓		✓				✓
WASHING MACHINE								✓			✓
DISHWASHER								✓			✓
SINK								✓			
BASEMENT	✓	✓	✓	✓	✓	✓	✓	✓	✓	✓	✓
GROUND FLOOR	✓	✓	✓	✓	✓	✓	✓	✓	✓	✓	✓
UPPER FLOOR	✓	✓	✓	✓	✓	✓	✓	✓	✓	✓	✓
LOFT/ATTIC	✓	✓	✓	✓	✓	✓	✓	✓	✓	✓	✓
PUMPS UP (METRES)	4	4	5	5	4	4	5	5	3	5	6
PUMPS ALONG (METRES)	50	40	100	100	40	40	100	50	30	100	100
DISCHARGE (MILLIMETRES)	22	22	22	22	22	22	22	32	32	22	22/32

BATHROOM ELECTRICS

Zones

The previous IEE 16th Edition identified zones within the bathroom to illustrate what type of electrics in the bathroom can be used or installed, and these have been updated in the 17th Edition. These zones take into account windows, doors, walls ceilings and partitions, assessing the level of risk in each zone, with specific requirements governing the type of equipment deemed safe to be used in each. Zones 0–2 are considered the wettest, and the former zone 3 is no longer defined.

<img src='/neweys/images/site/Editorial/knowledge/electricity-bathroom-iee-zones.png' width='610' height='416' alt='IEE Wiring Regulation Zones' title='IEE Wiring Regulation Zones' />

Zone 0

Applies to inside the bath or shower. Here electrical products must be low voltage (a maximum of 12V) and be IPX7, i.e. can withstand total accidental immersion.

Zone 1

Applies to the area around the bath or shower up to a height of 2.25m above the floor and at a radius of 1.2m from the water outlet. A minimum rating of IPX4 is required. If the fitting is 240V a 30mA residual current device (RCD) must also be used to protect the circuit in this zone, i.e. SELV with the transformer located beyond zone 2.

Zone 2

Applies to the area beyond Zones 0 and 1, 0.6m horizontally and up to 2.25m vertically, including any recessed window with a sill next to the bath. This area requires electrical products to be IPX4 or better, or SELV with the transformer located beyond zone 2. It is advisable to consider the area around a wash basin, within a 60cm radius of any tap as Zone 2.

Outside Zones

These are classed as anywhere outside Zones 0, 1 and 2 (subject to specific limits) and where no water jet is likely to be used. No IP rating is required here unless water jets are used for cleaning purposes in Zones 1, 2 and "Outside Zones", in which case a minimum IPX5 must be used.

Portable equipment is allowed in Outside Zones providing they are located where their flex length prevents them from being used in Zone 2, and they must be plugged in outside the bathroom, with the socket far enough away to ensure the appliance cannot be used inside zone 3.

Any space under the bath is considered out of scope, so long as it cannot be accessed without using tools such as a screwdriver.

Typical electrical products in bathrooms

Guidance for common electrical bathroom items with IP numbers includes:

Showers and Instant Water Heaters

Should be rated IPX4 or above and user safety should also be considered, i.e. installing appropriate thermostats and cut-outs to provide protection from rapid changes in water temperature. Instant demand electric showers must be supplied direct from the consumer unit.

Extractor fans

IPX4 or above and installed in Zone 2 with the SELV source located beyond Zone 2 located in Zone 3 or beyond. If this is not possible, a 230V IPX4 fan can be installed in Zone 1, but must be protected by a 30 mA Residual Current Device (RCD). This type of fan can be used in Zone 2 without an RCD. Where the fan has a timer trigger input, a 3-pole isolator is necessary to disconnect both poles.

Heating

Central heating is the safest, however if you need to use an electric heater, it must be fixed at a safe distance from the bath or shower. Electric and gas water heaters must be fixed and permanently wired and NEVER supplied via a plug and socket outlet.

Under Floor Heating

This is allowed in any zone, as per regulation 601–09–04 but must be covered by an earthed metallic grid. SELV supplied heating equipment can be used in Zone 1 but it is good practice to install it in Zone 2.

Heated Towel Rails

These are subject to BS EN 60335–2–43 (2003) which requires an IP rating of at least IPX1, however, if they are situated in Zone 2 the rating must be at least IPX4.

Lighting in bathrooms

This is subject to strict legislation, as per Section 701 of BS7671:2008, and should be IPX4 or above. Lights with a cord pull switch are not usually IP rated and should adhere to BS 3676 and be installed in Zone 3, the safest option being a ceiling mounted pull switch with the cord manufactured from insulating material. Some types of lights can be installed in Zone 0

(specifically for use in shower enclosures) but they must be 12V SELV. Portable lights are not allowed and lighting designed specifically for showers must be carefully fitted according to the instructions.

Electricity in the bathroom requires extra vigilance as not only does water conduct electricity well but an electric shock caused by the combination of water and electricity is more lethal as wet skin reduces the body's resistance to shock. Therefore it is absolutely vital that bathroom electrics are installed according to all relevant legislation.

Sockets

Sockets are not allowed in bathrooms or shower rooms (apart from shaver-supply units) unless they can be fitted at least three metres from the bath or shower.

Electrical shaver points must be a safe distance (in meters) from the bath or shower to avoid splashes

KEY TO ZONES

ZONE 0   ZONE 1   ZONE 2

60 cm

60 cm

60cm

60 cm

75cm

225 cm

2   ZONE 1   2

225 cm

2

60cm

225 cm   2   ZONE 1   2

225 cm

ZONE 0

ZONE 0

Explanation of IP Ratings for Protection

0	Not Protected	0	Not Protected
1	Protected against Solid Objects greater than 50mm	1	Protected against Dripping Water
2	Protected against Solid Objects greater than 12mm	2	Protected against Dripping Water when tilted to 15°
3	Protected against Solid Objects greater than 2.5mm	3	Protected against Spraying Water
4	Protected against Solid Objects greater than 1mm	4	Protected against Splashing Water
5	Dust Protected	5	Protected against Water Jets
6	Dust Tight	6	Protected against Heavy Seas
		7	Protected against the effects of Immersion
		8	Protected against Submersion

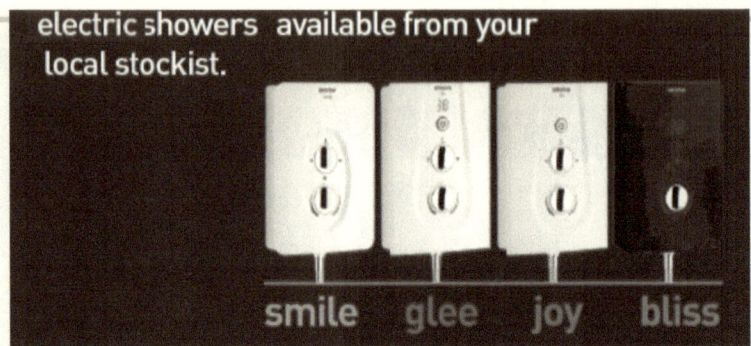

electric showers available from your local stockist.

smile   glee   joy   bliss

Instantaneous electric shower

An Instantaneous Electric Shower typically provides a hot shower with water at mains pressure. The basic, mains fed installation is shown to the right. It is generally fairly easy to install an Instantaneous Electric Shower as it usually only requires a cold water feed from the rising main and a suitable electrical connection - note however that Part P of the Building Regulations apply and a suitably qualified electrician must normally connect the shower unit as it will usually be

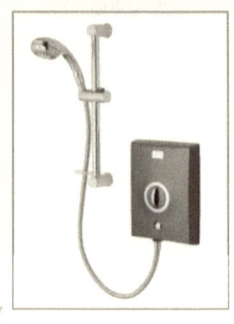

Electric showers explained

Electric showers heat the water as you go, meaning they only need a cold water supply to work and are ready to go without you having to heat water first. This can be good for your energy bills, as no unnecessary water heating goes on, and it's a real bonus if your boiler breaks down.

Electric showers should be installed by a professional

On the downside, electric showers do tend to have a weaker flow than mixer and power showers, although some come with an integral pump to help to combat this problem. You also need to watch out for limescale build-up - a common problem with electric showers.

The power of electric showers is generally between 8.5kW and 10.8kW - the higher the value, the more powerful the shower. It's best to get your electric shower installed by an expert as the high-power electrical element needs to be connected to a separate fused electrical supply circuit. To find out more, read our guide on how to install an electric shower.

With regular electric showers, the water may get very hot if the cold water supply is being used elsewhere in your house. Thermostatic electric showers can control the water temperature to within about 1-2°C of the temperature you need, so they're a better bet if other people or appliances often use water when you're having a shower.

Pros of electric showers: only needs a cold water supply, you don't pay to heat water that doesn't get used, cheaper to buy than other types, still works if your boiler breaks down

Cons of electric showers: generally a weaker flow than other types of shower, limescale build-up can be a problem, professional installation can be pricey

Cost of electric showers: anywhere from £50 for a basic 8.5kW model to around £400 for a sleek, 10.5kW version

Maximum Shower Rating (kW)	Maximum load (Amps)	Recommended Minimum Cable Size (Twin core and earth mm²)	Maximum size of Protective Device (Amps)
6.0	26	6	32
6.5	29	6	32
7.0	31	6	32
7.5	33	10	40
8.0	35	10	40
8.5	37	10	40
9.0	39	10	40
9.5	42	10	45
10.0	44	10	45
10.5	46	16	50
11.0	48	16	50

Shower Pumps

Shower Booster Pumps

• New improved shower pumps
• Improved quality and reliability
• Quiet operation

CE WRAS

Negative Head Systems

A negative head system exists when there is insufficient pressure or head of water under gravity to provide a flow / pressure at the outlet. Typically a negative head condition exists where the flow from the outlet is less than 1 litre/min.

Positive Head Systems

A positive head system exists when sufficient pressure is available under gravity to provide a flow at the outlet. Typically a positive head condition exists where the flow from the outlet is more than 1 litre/min.

Pressures

Pumps are rated in 'bar' which is the measure of pressure, 1 bar pressure being equal to 10 metres static head of water. Generally the higher the bar rating the higher the performance. However it is important to match the correct size of pump with the application to ensure optimum performance.

The following can be used as a general guide for applications:

1.0 bar pressure
1.5 – 3.0 bar pressure 3.0 bar pressure +

Twin pumps

= = =

Low boost Medium boost High boost

Twin pumps are designed to boost both hot and cold water supplies equally.

Single pumps

Single pumps are designed to boost single water supplies; hot, cold or pre- mixed.

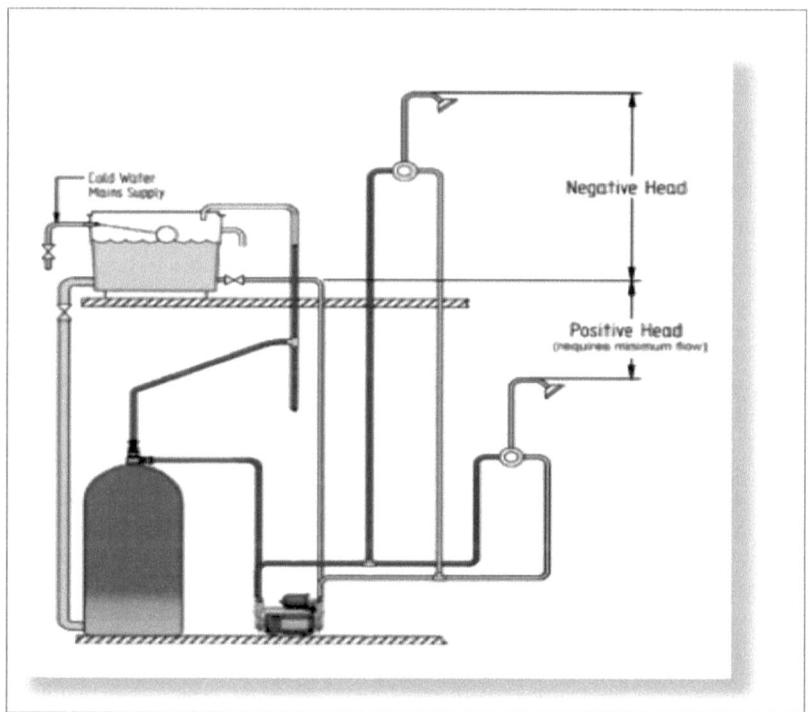

Install Shower Pumps

There are many ways to install a shower pump, however, there are certain rules that will work for all shower pumps, no matter which make or model.

Below you will find basic guidelines to demonstrate how to install a twin impellor pump, pumping both your hot and cold water supplies to a shower valve.

If you need specific pump details you can now download the installation instructions for each model on the individual product pages (see our shower pump collection here), you may also want to have a look at our Pump Comparison Guide showing the key features of each model.

Cold Water Supplies and Connections.

First rule of thumb is to make sure that you are storing enough cold water for the shower. 225 litres or 50 gallons is normally adequate for most showering applications.

Next consider the position of the pump it should always be fitted with at least 600mm from the bottom of the cold water storage tank to the top of the pump motor / impellor casing. As shown in our drawing

the best position for the pump is at the base of the hot water cylinder and as close as possible to the cylinder.

The installation of the water supply from the cold water storage tank to your pump is straight forward. Use a separate 22mm outlet connection from the cold water storage tank, we recommend this is drilled on the opposite side of the tank to the float valve (to make this connection use a 22mm compression tank connector).

It is good plumbing practice to next fit a 22mm full bore isolating valve in your new cold water supply pipe. You should always include a way of isolating the water supplies both at source and locally to the pump you are installing (please refer to our drawing).

This supply can now feed the pump inlet, if there are no isolating valves fitted to the pump anti-vibration couplers (the flexible pump connectors) then fit them just prior to the pump. It is important to note that all our pumps are supplied complete with av-couplers.

It does not matter whether the pump has 22mm or 15mm connections, by supplying the pump with a 22mm supply complete with the full bore valves the suction side of the pump will not be restricted.

Hot Water Supplies and Connections.

The best position for the pump is at the base of the hot water cylinder as close as possible to the cylinder. There are many described ways of connecting to a hot water cylinder, but there is one way that is the best. We recommend you install a separate connection that is not restricted and ensures that little air can get into the pump impellors. It is important to note that excessive air will damage the pump.

With this in mind use a dedicated flange to connect to the hot water cylinder. A non stop Essex flange will give the least resistance and is best for 22mm pumps, if you are fitting a 15mm pump a Surrey or a Salamander S-Flange will be sufficient.

Assuming you have followed this advice then you will only need to fit 1 separate full bore isolating valve to the supply pipe as your pump will be within reaching distance of the cylinder.

Flush Pipe Work Prior To Connecting to the Pump

Once you have connected the supply pipes to the pump it is now time to prime the pump. Firstly, with the electrical supply off run one bucket of water out of both the hot and the cold sides of the pump until the water has run clear and there is no apparent air.

You can now run the pipes to the shower valve, if the pump has 22mm connections then it is best practice to run 22mm pipe close to the shower valve. If the pump has 15mm connections then run your pipe in 15mm. Please Note: If the pipes from your pump to the shower run back up to the loft then you will need to fit air vents in the highest pipe position.

You should fit isolating valves in an accessible position close to the shower valve for servicing, now flush your pipes again prior to connecting the shower valve. Then make your connections to your shower.

That's it happy showering.........

What is a good shower?

Some people will be happy with a 7.2 KW electric shower heating water to 30 degrees centigrade which will give you 3.5 litres a minute, whilst others consider 4.0 litres a minute the absolute minimum for a good shower in winter.

A 'good' shower by traditional UK standards is 6 litres a minute

In the USA the maximum flow permitted from a shower head is 9.5 litres a minute and the UK government is looking to bring in an even lower rate of perhaps 8 or 9 litres a minute.

A typical UK Power Shower will give 12+ litres a minute and to achieve the lower flows, in common with the USA, manufacturers in the UK will put in flow restrictors in the shower head kill the power of the power shower to reduce the flow and pressure.

In Summary:-

3.5 litres a minute – 7.2 KW electric shower heating the water 30 degrees centigrade

4.0 litres a minute – is often perceived as the minimum flow for an adequate shower in winter

4.7 litres a minute – 9.8 KW electric shower heating water 30 degrees centigrade

6.0 litres a minute is a good shower by traditional UK standards

4.5 to 6.5 litres a minute is the typical output from a showerpowerbooster

9.5 litres a minute is the maximum permitted flow for a shower in the USA

12+ litres a minute is the typical output of a UK Power Shower (can be reduced by killing flow and pressure with a flow regulator)

50+ litres a minute is required for many top Continental body jet showers

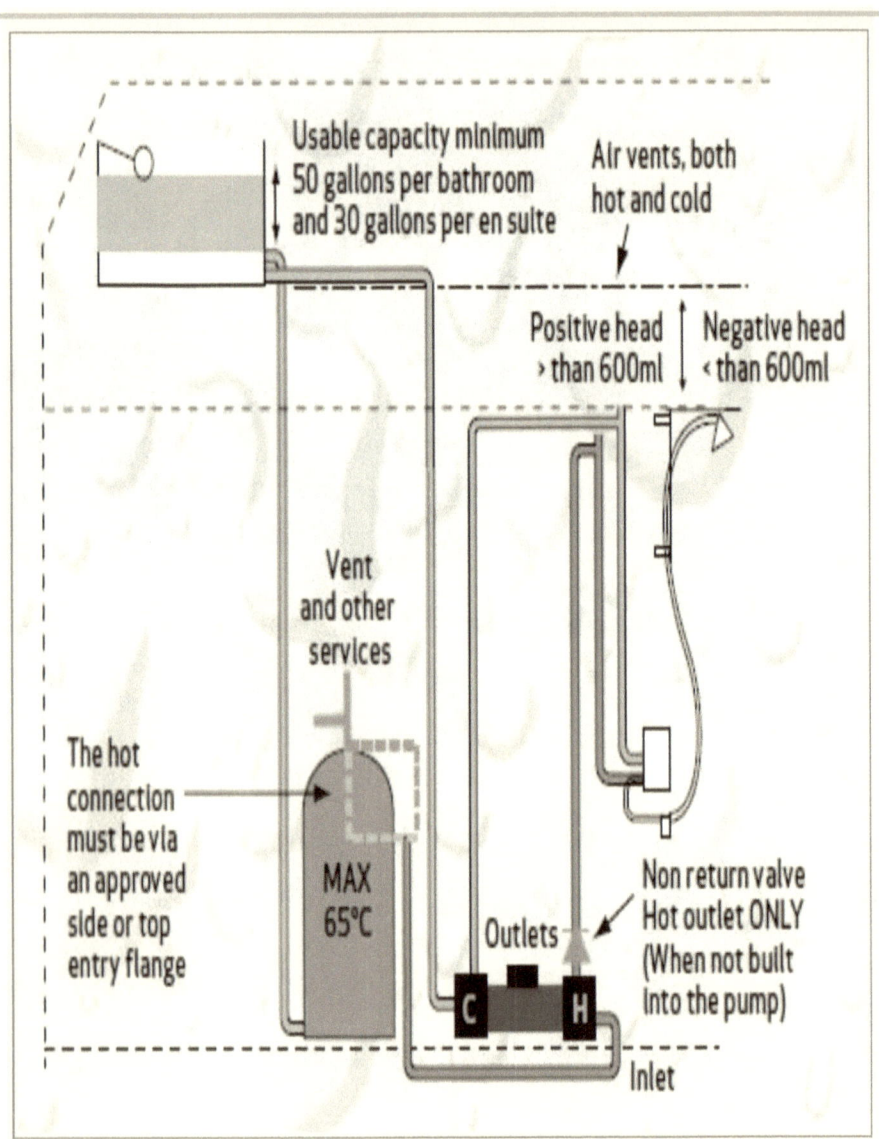

Usable capacity minimum 50 gallons per bathroom and 30 gallons per en suite

Air vents, both hot and cold

Positive head › than 600ml   Negative head ‹ than 600ml

Vent and other services

The hot connection must be via an approved side or top entry flange

MAX 65°C

Outlets

C   H

Non return valve Hot outlet ONLY (When not built into the pump)

Inlet

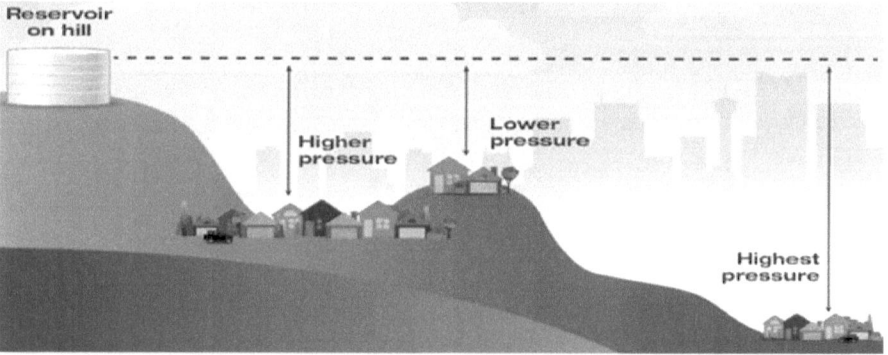

To understand the technicalities of bath-room plumbing and installation it is necessary to understand the meaning of water pressure and its effect on the bathroom and its enjoyment.

There are a couple of simple figures to appreciate. Firstly what is the expression of Head of Water and what is a bar. Basically it is a measure of atmospheric pressure and in this context

1 bar = approximately 10 metres or in imperial terms 33 feet. But what does head of water actually mean. There is some varia-

tion in its interpretation but it is important to understand the normal bathroom meaning of this term.

On the following pages we have provided diagrams and tables to clarify these points.

This shows the measurement of head of water in relation to the supply to a shower pump. In this case the level of the water in the supply tank is shown as the point from which the head is measured. Although this is teechnically correct this is not the way we measure it for bathroom purposes

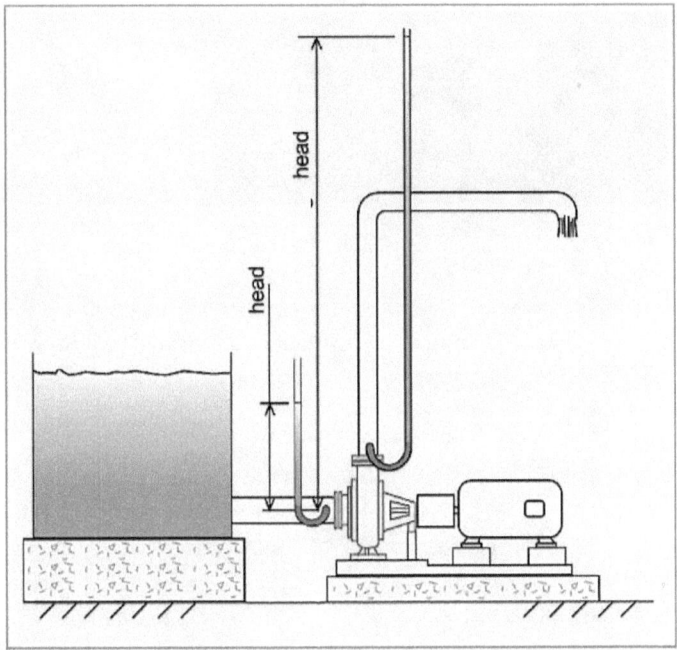

This is the measurement used for bathroom purposes. Measuring to the bottom of the tank gives a certain margin of safety assuming the level will not be constant.

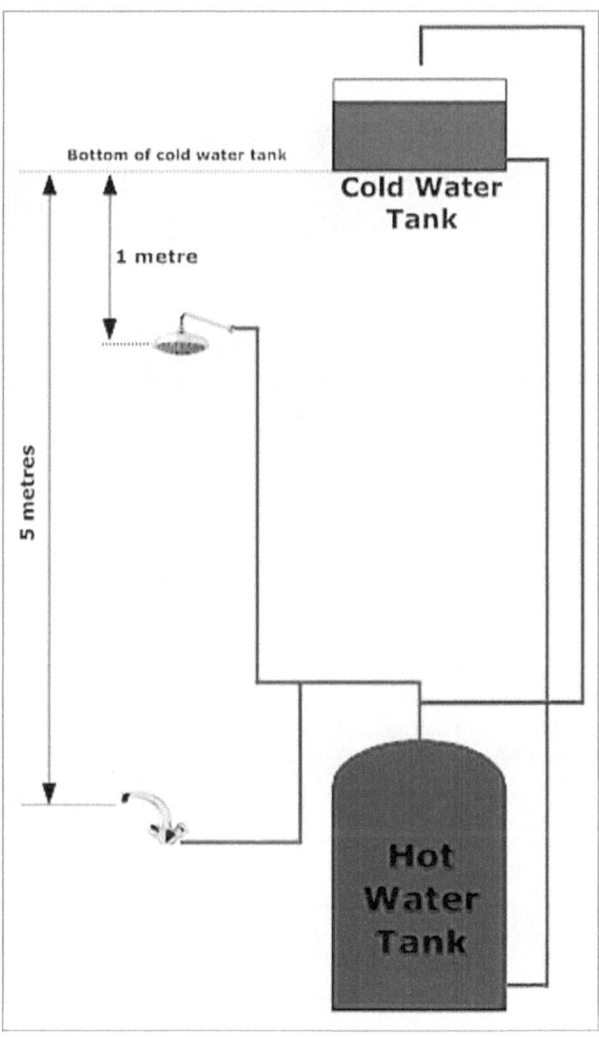

These illustrations show the definition of head in terms of pressure wit the varying hot water systems

Hot Gravity & Cold Gravity/Mains

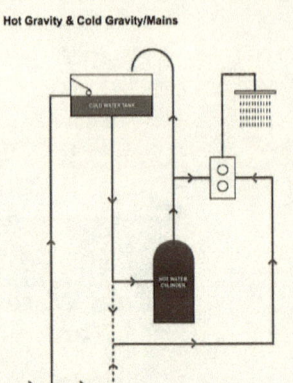

Combination Boiler

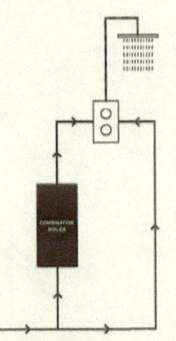

Low pressure systems (LP 0.1-2 bar)

✓ You have a cold water storage tank in the loft.
✓ You have a hot water cylinder.
✓ You do not have a shower pump installed.

If all of the above apply to your home you can choose any product marked with LP (minimum 0.2 bar).

Note A gravity fed system provides MP (0.5 bar) to fittings downstairs in a 2 story property where the cold water tank is in the loft.

Medium pressure systems (MP 0.5-1 bar)

✓ You have a combination boiler that heats water on demand.
✓ You do not have any storage tanks.
✓ You do not have a shower pump installed.

If all of the above apply to your home you can choose any product marked with LP, MP or HP1.

Mains High Pressure

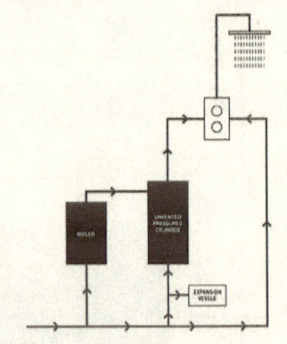

Pump Assisted

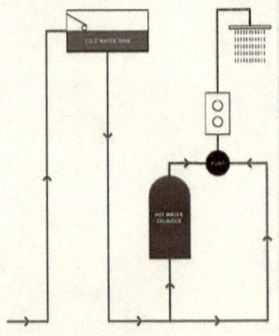

High pressure systems (HP1/2/3 2-3 bar)

✓ You have an unvented cylinder with an expansion cylinder.
✓ You have no cold water tank in the loft.

If either of the above apply to your home you can choose any product marked LP, MP, HP1, HP2 and HP3 (minimum 1/2/3 bar).

High pressure systems (MP to HP4)

✓ You have a booster pump fitted.

If either of the above apply to your home you can choose any of our products. **Please check your pump meets the minimum pressure.**

This table shows the relation of head of water to the actual pressure.

Pressure (lb/in**2)	Head (ft)									
	0	1	2	3	4	5	6	7	8	9
0	0.0	2.3	4.6	6.9	9.2	11.6	13.9	16.2	18.5	20.8
10	23.1	25.4	27.7	30.0	32.3	34.7	37.0	39.3	41.6	43.9
20	46.2	48.5	50.8	53.1	55.5	57.8	60.1	62.4	64.7	67.0
30	69.3	71.6	73.9	76.2	78.6	80.9	83.2	85.5	87.8	90.1
40	92.4	94.7	97.0	99.4	102	104	106	109	111	113
50	116	118	120	122	125	127	129	132	134	136
60	139	141	143	146	148	150	152	155	157	159
70	162	164	166	169	171	173	176	178	180	183
80	185	187	189	192	194	196	199	201	203	206
90	208	210	213	215	217	220	222	224	226	229

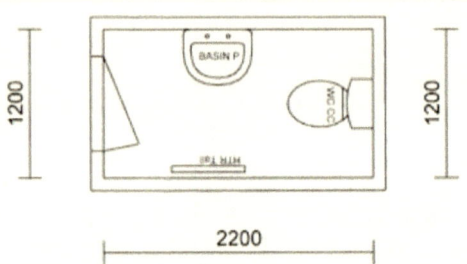

5

CLOAKROOM

It is quite rare to be asked to design a cloakroom but as part of a whole house plumbing remodeling it is a distinct possibility. You may also be asked within this context to design a full cloakroom including the plumbing possibilities. You can install a cloakroom almost anywhere in the property but often only with the benefit of a macerator. As a cloakroom is usually for guests it will often be in a less sensitive part of the building where noise is not a bit problem.

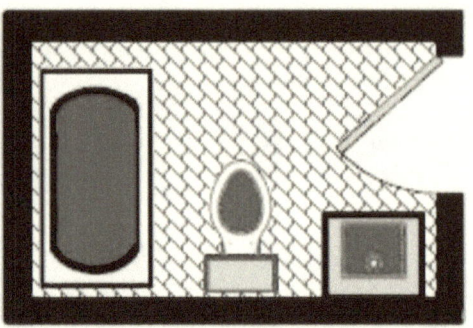

6

PRESENTATION

OK you have planned the bathroom, now you have to sell it. There are many ways to present a project and with the larger projects it is wise to present at different stages. You would obviously start with a floor plan and show the customer a nice neat plan, perhaps a bit of rendering as the attached plan? Then you would proceed to a 3d plan, preferably hand drawn, but for simple bathrooms a computer 3d will do but for the larger projects most customers prefer a hand drawn and rendered 3d.

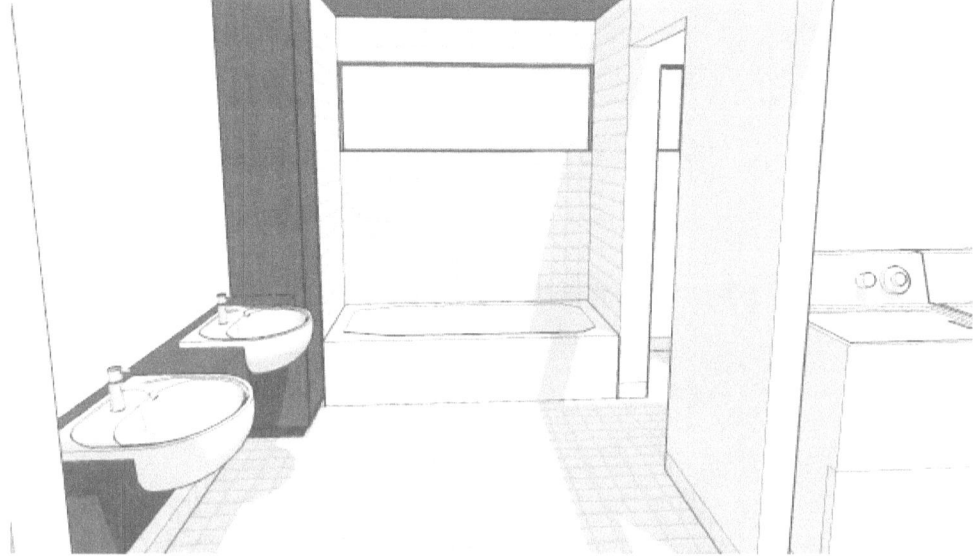

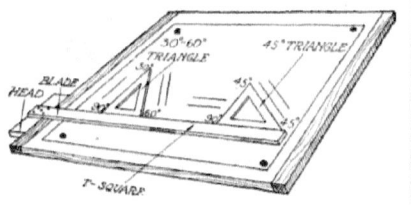

7

INTRODUCTION TO PERSPECTIVE

This is a new look at perspective especially for the paperback format which has a limited number of pages. This publication is all about perspectives and not about planning. We have already published various planning guides and we will be publishing a kitchen planning and perspective and a bathroom version. Please note this is a **MONOCHROME** version which allows us to offer a really comprehensive guide with **STEP BY STEP** instructions, at a very keen price

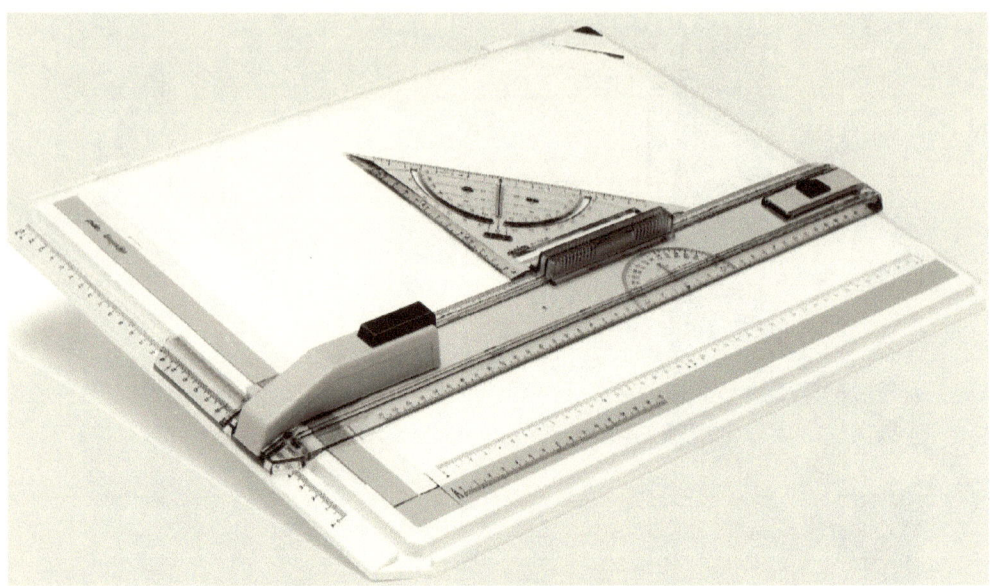

EQUIPMENT

It is best to start by familiarising yourself with the drawing instru-
ments. Don't worry if you cannot follow the drawing to begin
with. It will soon fall into place and you will start to see the perspective earlier and earlier at each attempt. When you handle
the pens or pencils don't make too hard an impression. In fact a
light stroke is the best technique but you may need to start a bit
heavier just to follow the process Lets start with the drawing
board, clearly many professionals will be using a full size drawing board but the A4 board is perfectly adequate for most purposes, Easy to carry around and simple to use.

You should find information supplied with the board but most of
them are similar. There is a fixed horizontal ruler which slides
up and down the board and has a lock (shown in red in this
case) You should not draw any lines unless the ruler is locked.
There are some big, famous German brands such as Rotring, offering products at competitive prices. Walk into any major sta-

tioners and you should find a selection.

The boards have a track around the edges so it can be used in portrait or landscape mode. Horizontal lines are drawn with the main sliding ruler. Vertical and angle lines are drawn using the set square. You can see the 45° set square in the illustration below.

To become proficient in all the basic techniques you will need a scale rule, a 45° and a 30° set square.

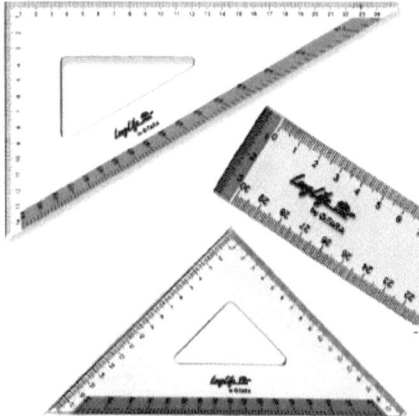

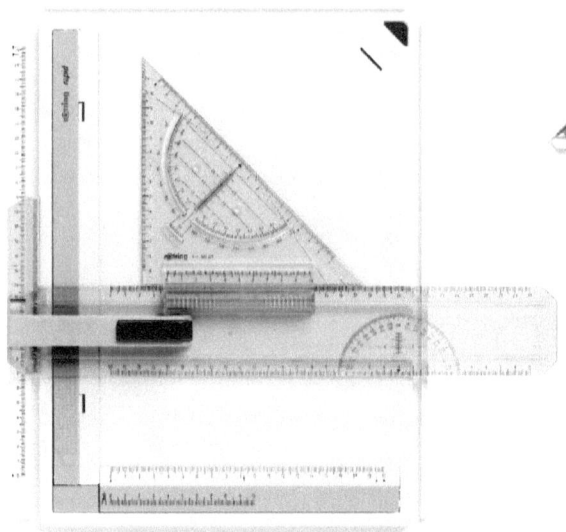

VARIATIONS OF 3D DRAWING

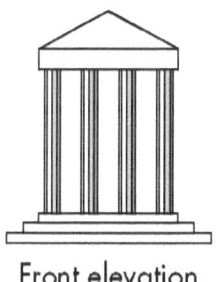

Front elevation

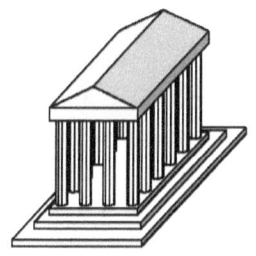

Elevation oblique

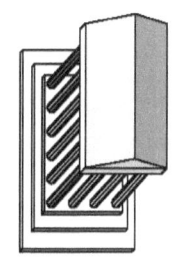

Plan oblique

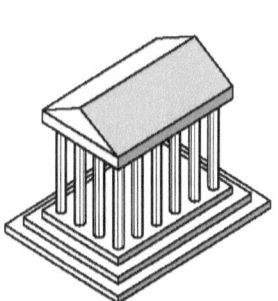

Isometric

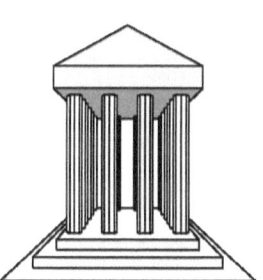

One-point perspective

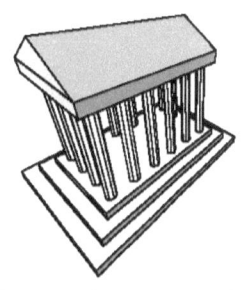

Three-point perspective

TYPES OF 3D DRAWING TECHNIQUES

There are a large number of techniques but the main ones we will be considering here are AXONOMETRIC, ISOMETRIC, 1 POINT PERSPECTIVE, 2 POINT PERSPECTIVE AND BIRD'S EYE PERSPECTIVE. Axonometric and Isometric are similar techniques but using 45° and 30° set squares respectively. These are both in scale whatever you draw. they are sometimes referred to as parallel perspective or planametric.

The other techniques are true perspectives using one vanishing point or two vanishing points. Only part of the drawing is in an actual scale. The rest of the dimensions - the projected dimensions - need to be calculated or found with the perspective ruler. We will discuss the perspective measurements later but first we need to look at the very quick, and simple techniques of Isometric and Axonometric.

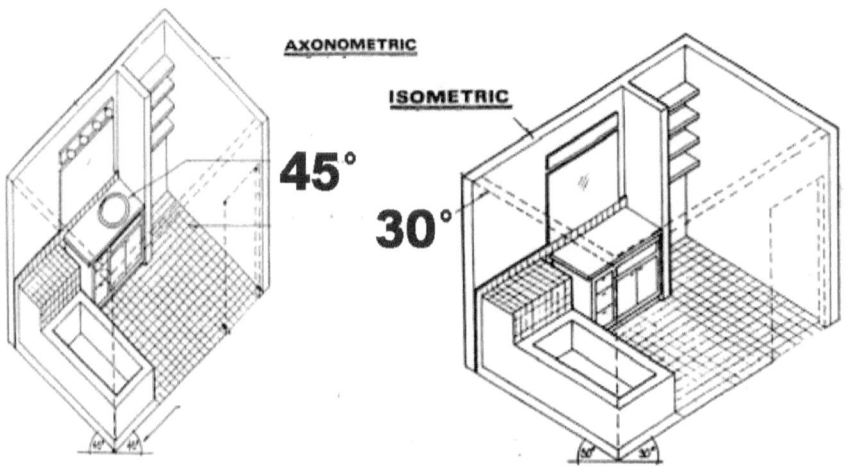

As you can see, the Axonometric method uses 90° vertical lines and 45° projection lines. the Isometric is virtually the same techniques but uses 30° projection lines.

Although both drawings above show bathrooms we have found that the Axonometric is easiest for bathrooms and the Isometric best for kitchens.

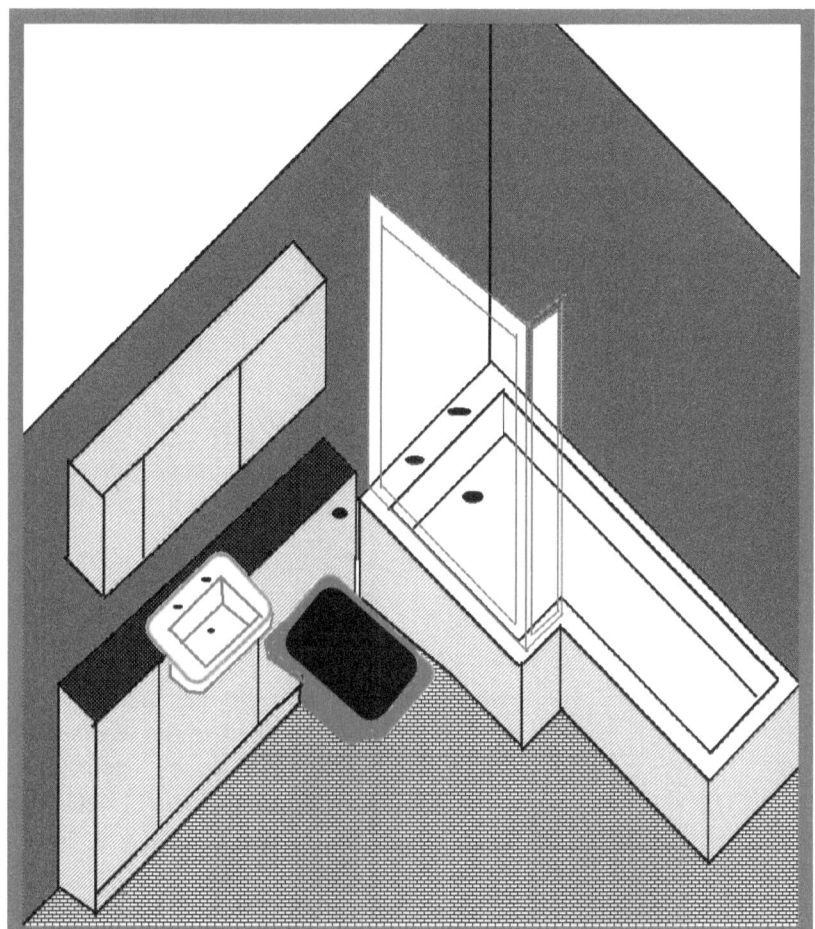

9

AXONOMETRIC & ISOMETRIC

Ok let's start drawing. Clearly we prefer to use a drawing board but you can use a simple drawing programme on a computer such as Adobe Illustrator or similar types which are often very cheap or even free. the choice is yours but if you have the dexterity for hand drawing you can produce a superior presentation - that's what it is all about

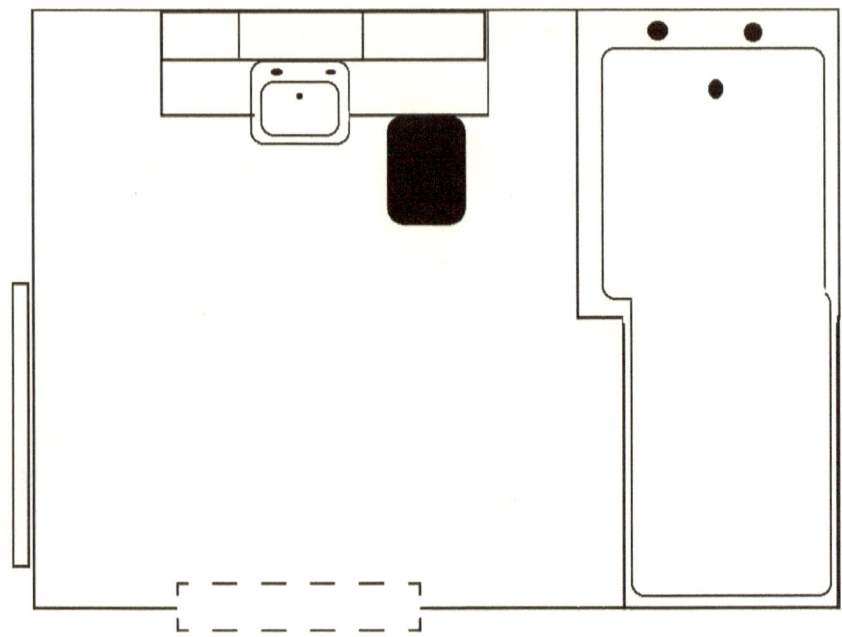

AXONOMETRIC
BATHROOM
METHOD

Now we will commence an Axonometric Bathroom example. Bathrooms have a lot of rounded shapes that are not easy to draw in 3d but by using some of the more geometric shapes we can at least commence to draw these shapes. You will find that you can employ this technique to show alternative products and as you continue practising your 3d you will perfect methods of drawing these awkward shapes.

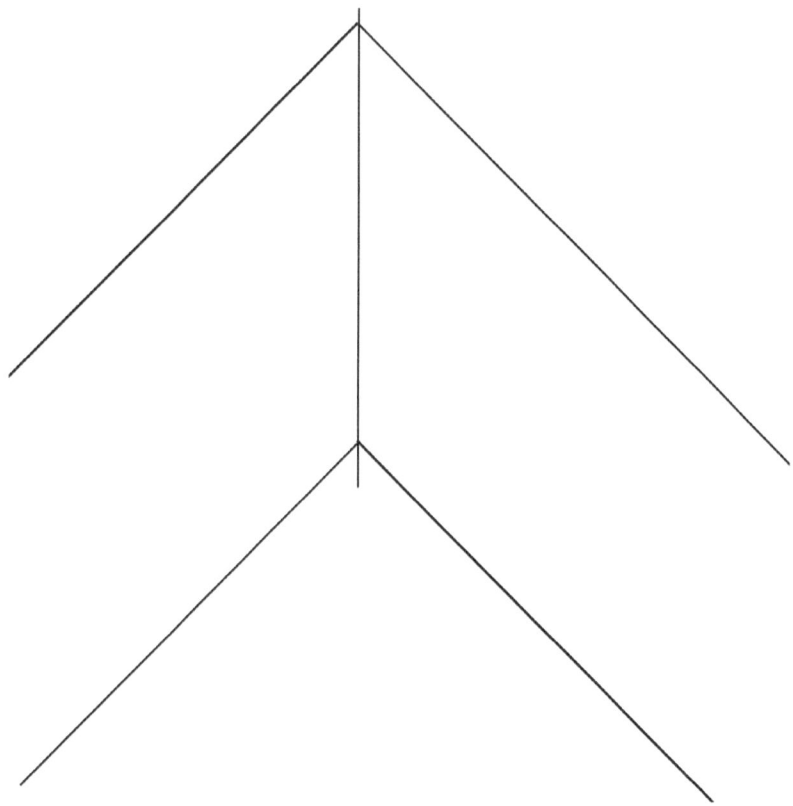

As before draw the
primary walls in
scale

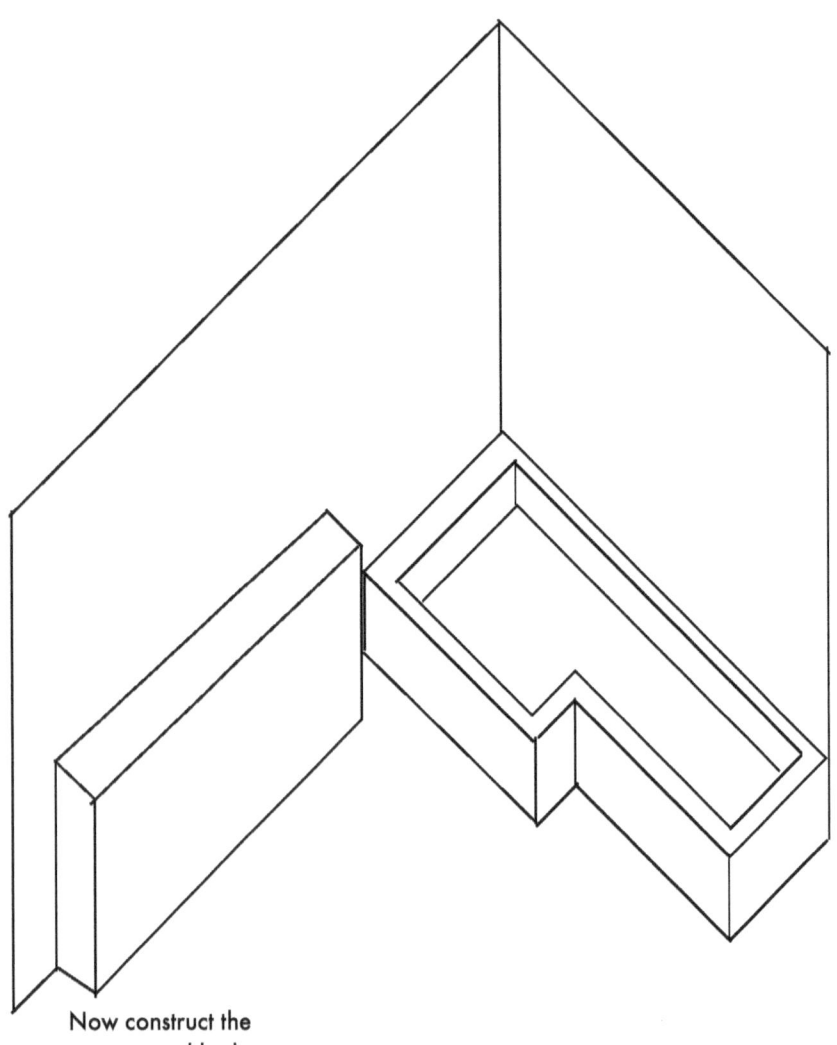

Now construct the
carcase and bath
outine using the
45° technique

Continue with the
carcassing and add
detail such as the
bath interior

continue with detail
and unit sizes etc

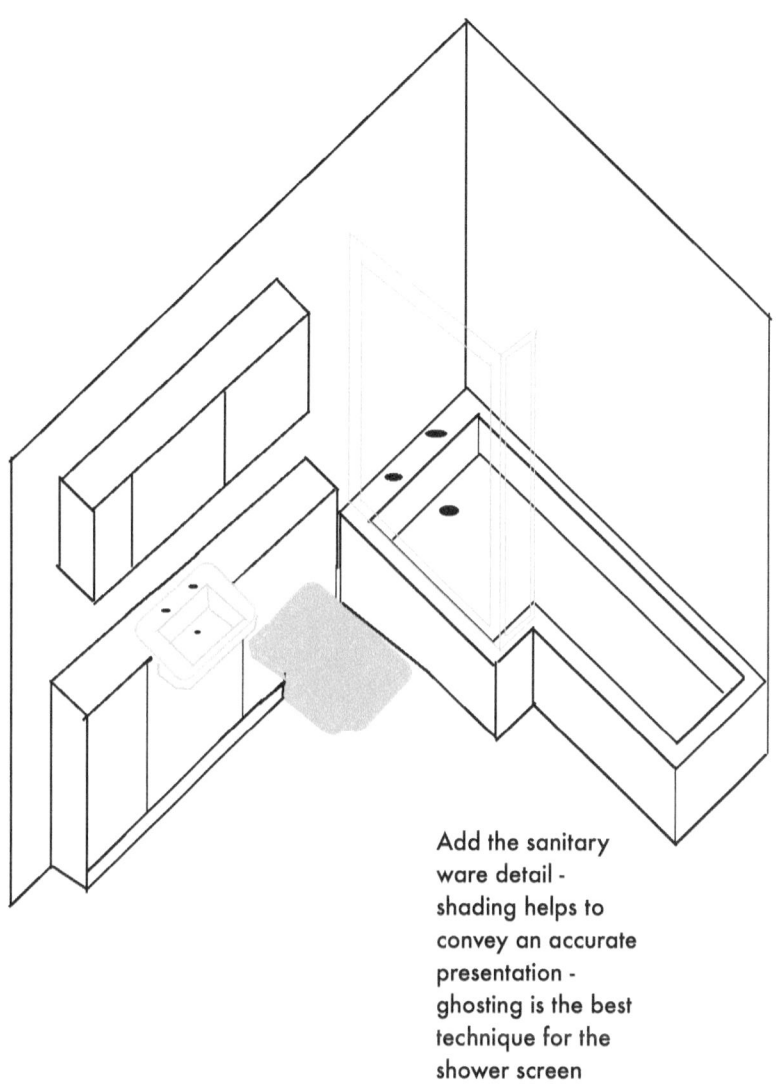

Add the sanitary
ware detail -
shading helps to
convey an accurate
presentation -
ghosting is the best
technique for the
shower screen

The final drawing
with some effective
rendering - looks
great in colour.

This is an actual
photo of the
bathroom we were
just drawing

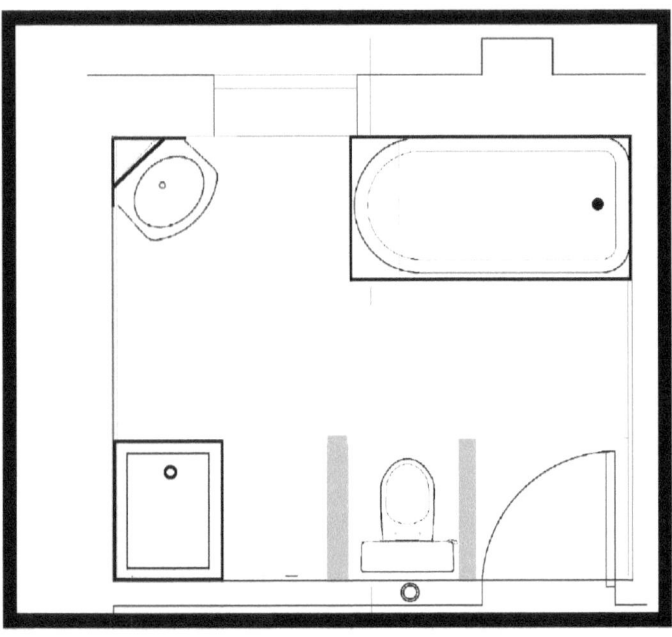

ISOMETRIC BATHROOM METHOD

This is essentially the same as the Axonometric method but using the 30/60° set square. You will soon learn when to use the 60° set square but you will also find it useful for things like cooker hood doors coming out from the wall unit line.

Always remember to start with a **SCALE PLAN** and draw everything in **ISOMETRIC** to the same scale throughout

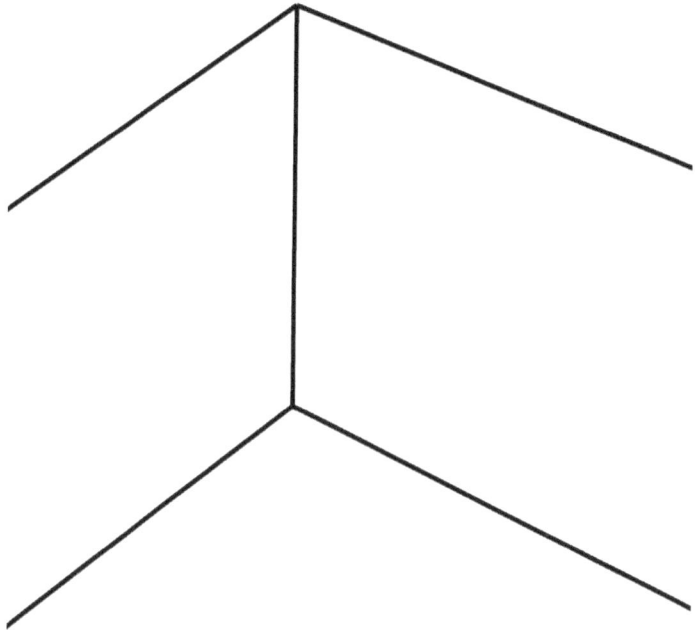

As with the
Axonometric
choose the corner
then draw the walls

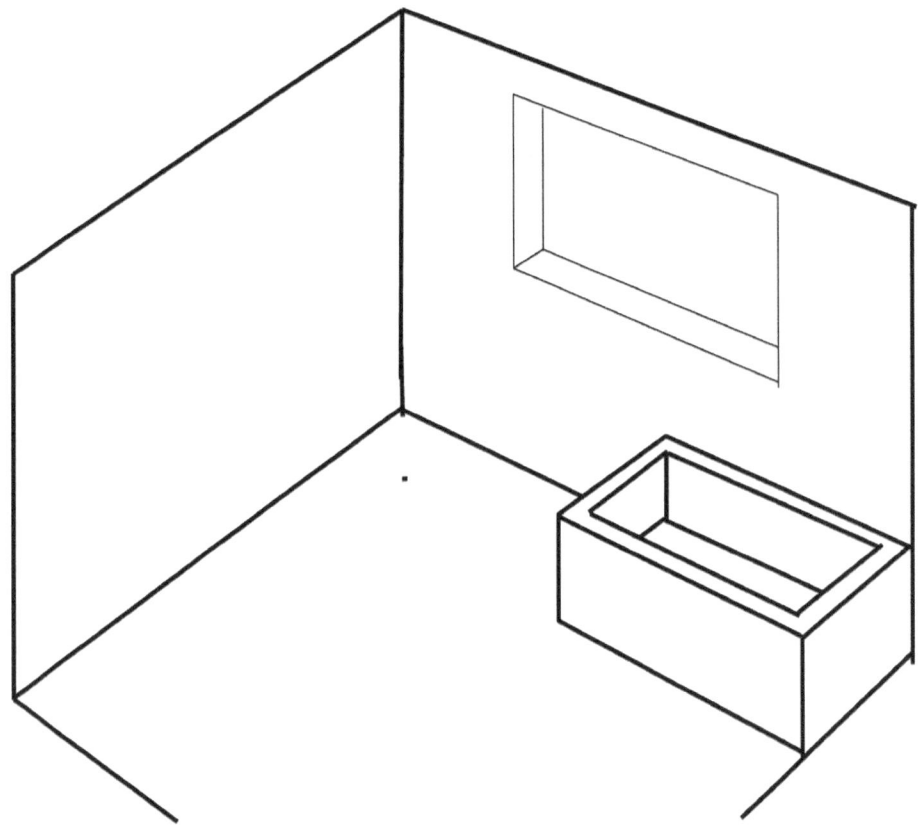

Then start laying
out the room - you
can use some
interpretation for
the actual fitments.

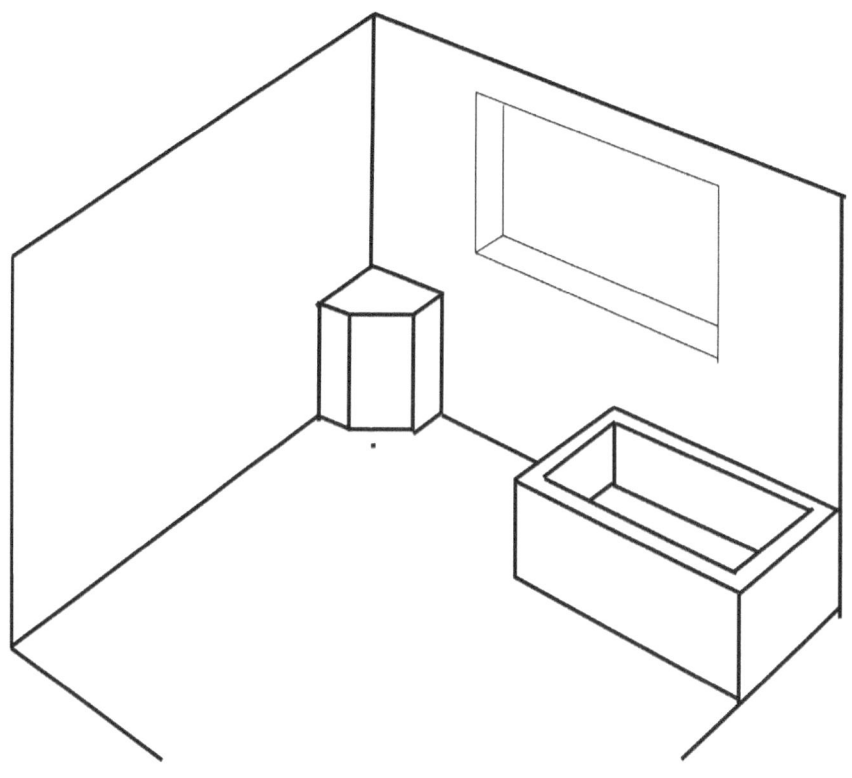

Continue with the
room - we have
chosen a
pentangle vanity
unit which is more
readily available..

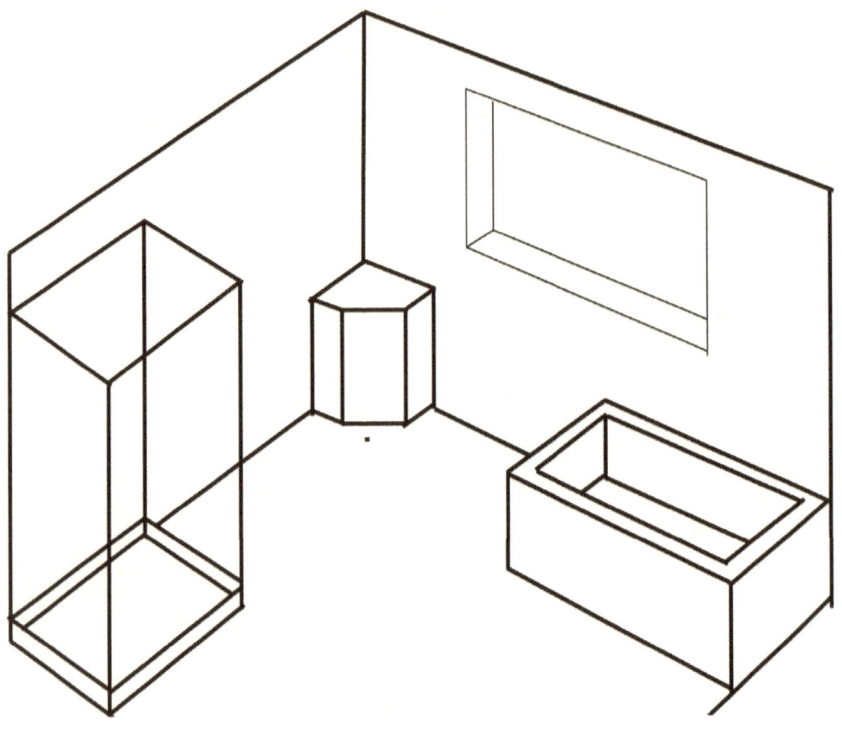

Now construct
shower outline on
the left hand wall.

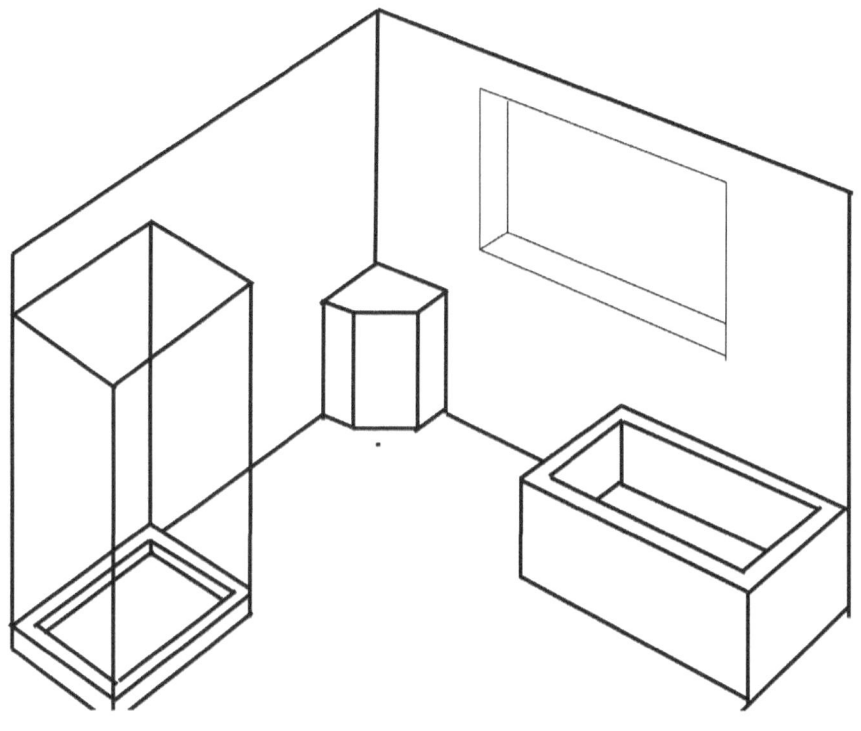

Continue with the
shower profiling
and detail

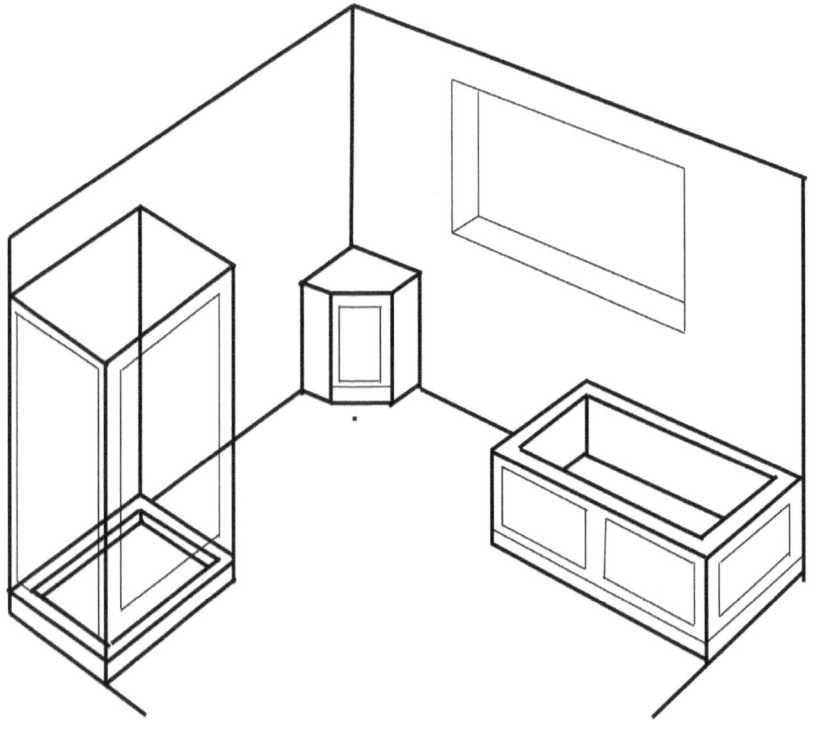

Continue with
detailing

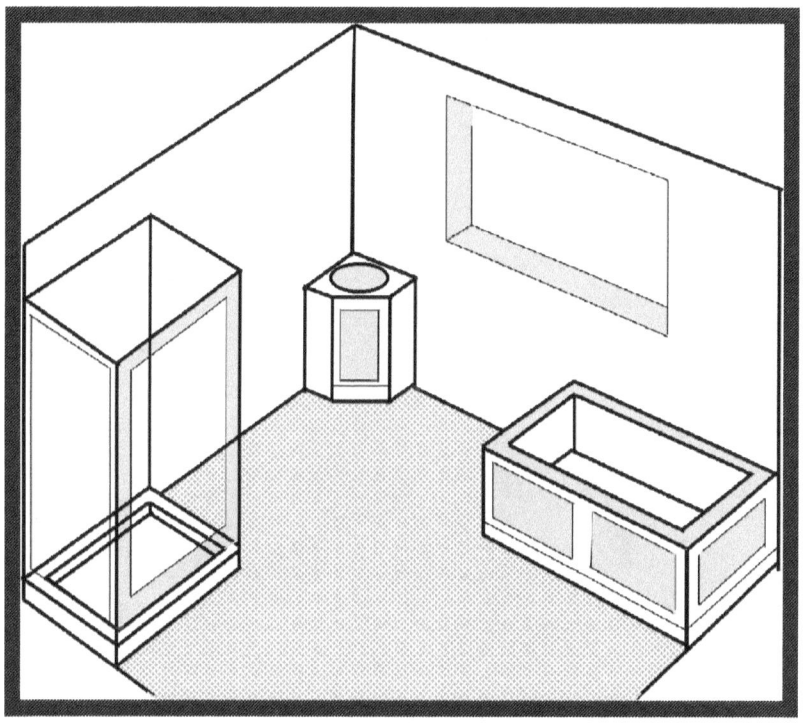

Tidy the drawing
removing hidden
lines, finish
profiling, rendering
and detailing

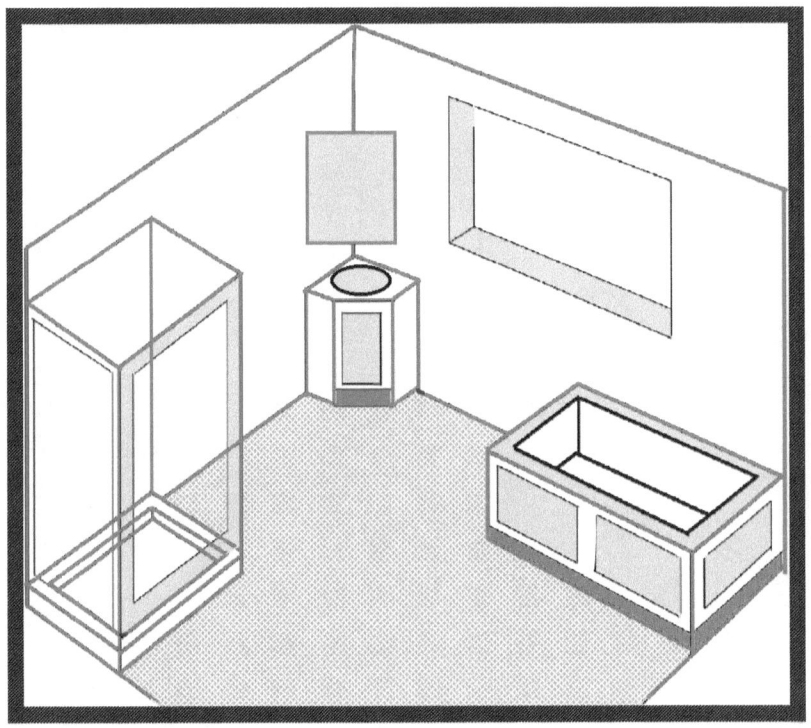

Add further details
as and if, required

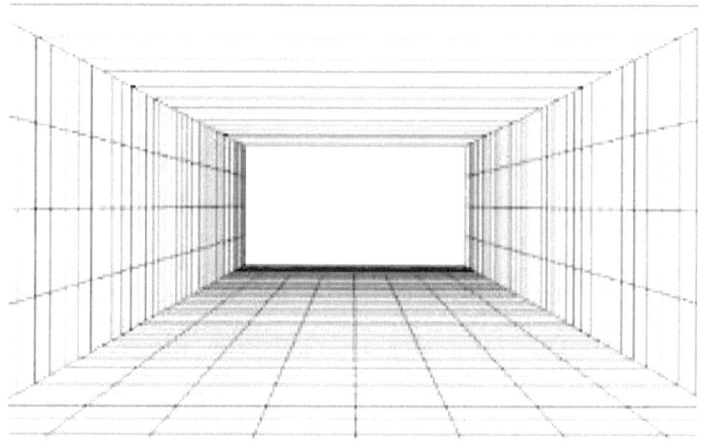

VANISHING POINT

10

The vanishing point is said to have been discovered, or should we say, introduced, in the 14th or 15th century. . I have to say that I am skeptical about this. The vanishing point is so obvious in drawings but more importantly in real life instances. Have a look at the railway line perspective. . OK there weren't any prehistoric railways but there surely were many instances that would have indicated the need and use of the vanishing point. It is perhaps well worth remembering that even Neanderthal man left some quite elaborate drawings the their dwelling caves??

In the past a lot of learners used to use the Perspective grid. We always found this very tedious, extremely restrictive and incredibly boring. It is, of course only usable for one discipline and unless you regularly use tracing paper it is a total waste of time. It is actually easier to draw properly, from scratch, and choose the view that suits the project and the drawing best.

You have probably guessed by now that 1 POINT PERSPECTIVE DRAWING uses one vanishing point. And, of course, 2 POINT PERSPECTIVE DRAWING uses two vanishing points.

You generally place your vanishing points on the horizon ine which is traditionally about eye level - around 1600 mm, but in reality you can choose anywhere but you need to choose the best place for your view. For interiors the standard placement is best. With a 1 point drawing you simply bias the vanishing point away from the longest wall so you can get the best view of that wall. With 2 point drawings you place the vanishing point as far away from the drawing as possible. Obviously with an A4 drawing board this doesn't give you much scope but a rule of thumb is to place it on the outside rim of the board.

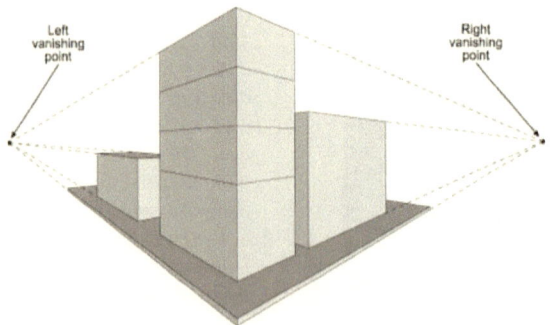

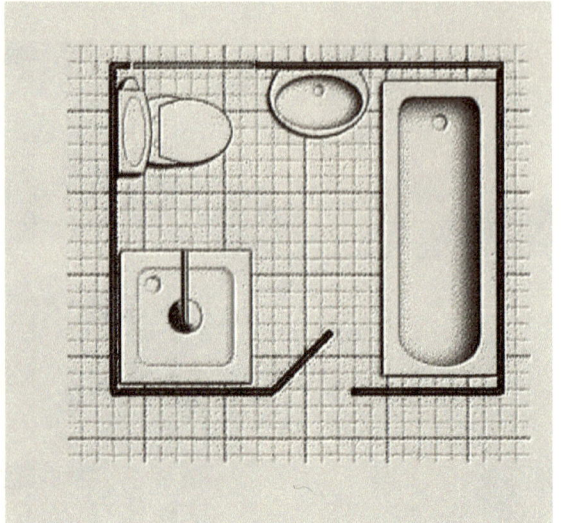

This is our plan but we have substituted a modern square sink and toilet:

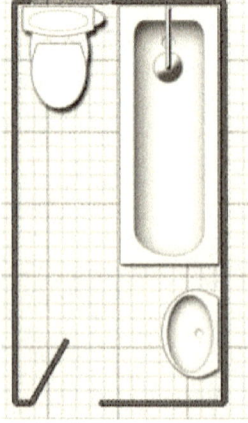

11

1 POINT PERSPECTIVE

BATHROOM METHOD

As with all 3d drawings start with a scale plan. As with the kitchen drawing you start with a back wall IN SCALE.

As before draw the
back wall IN
SCALE

X

Locate the
vanishing point for
your desired view

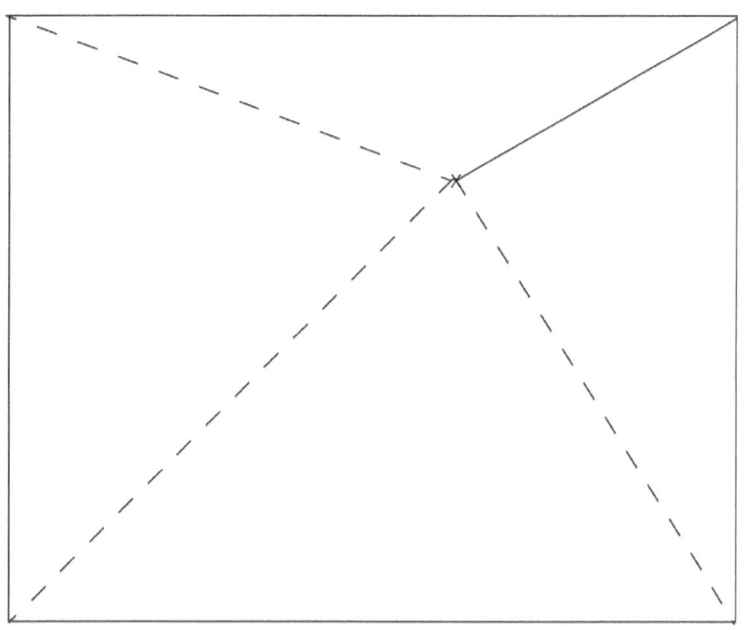

Line up the
vanishing point with
the four corners of
the back wall

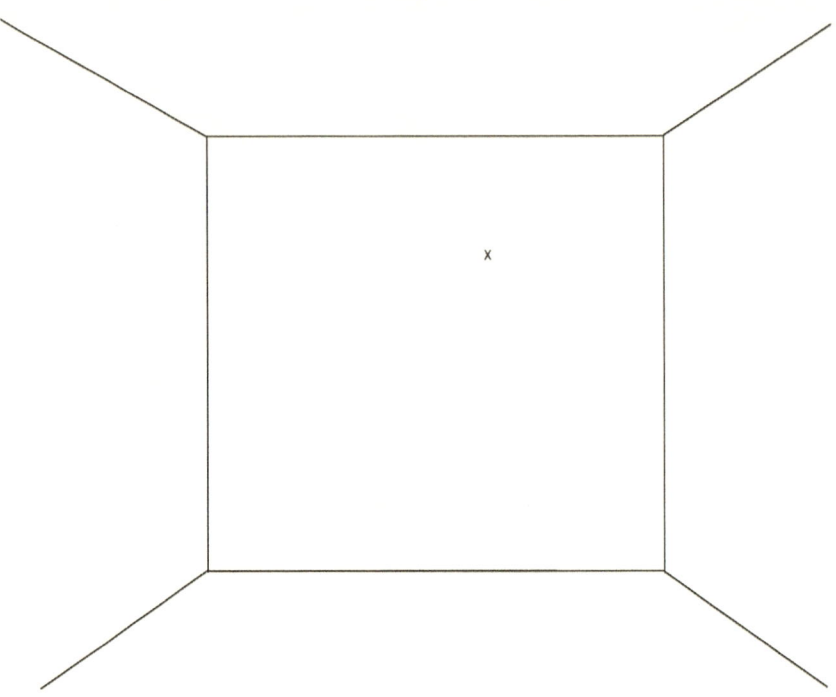

x

Project the four
corners

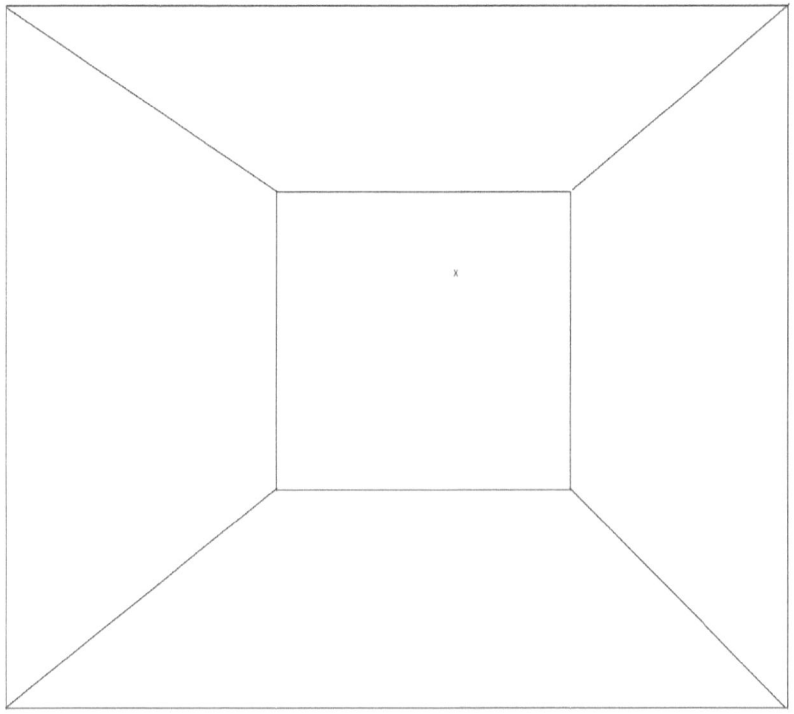

Square the room
using the space
available or your
perspective ruler

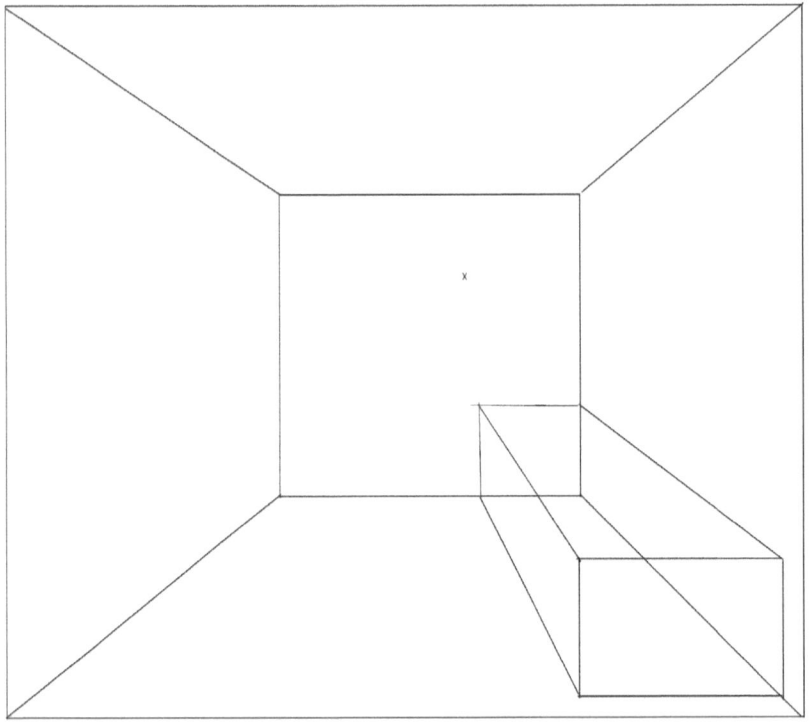

Start with the major
shapes such as the
bath

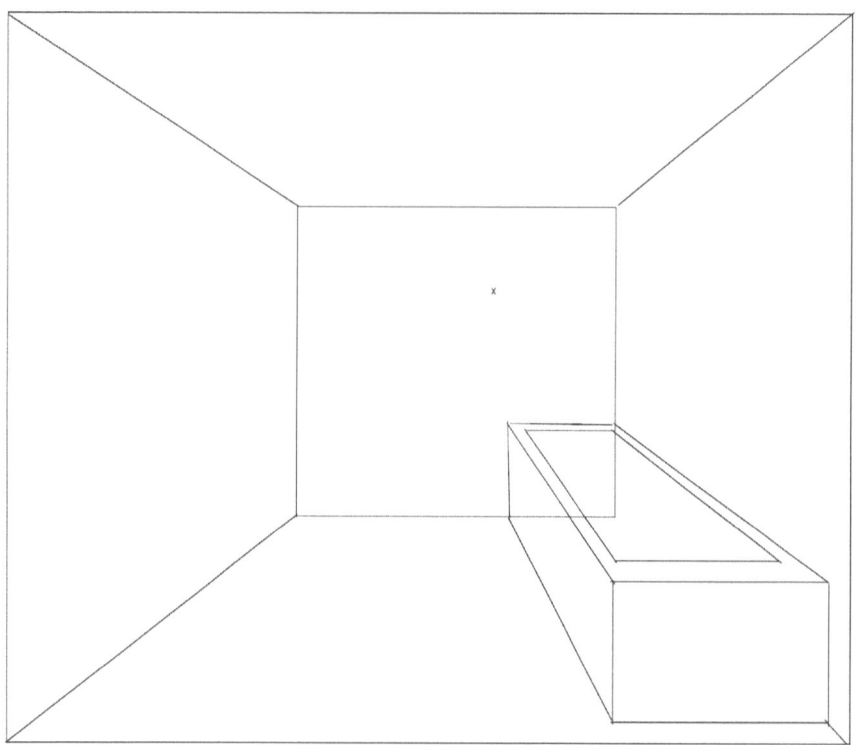

Add some detail

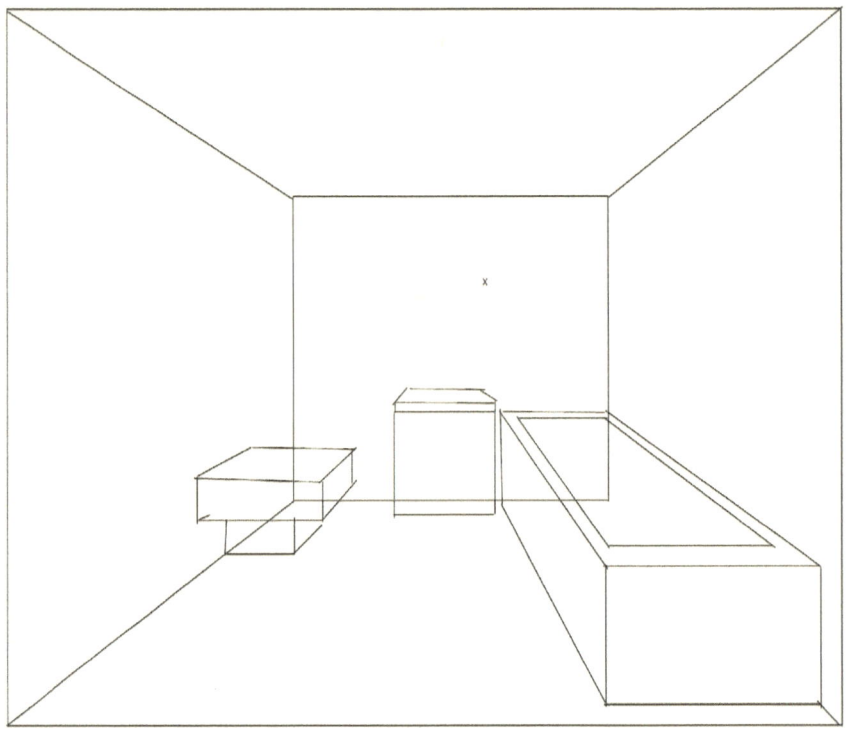

**Continue with the
shapes**

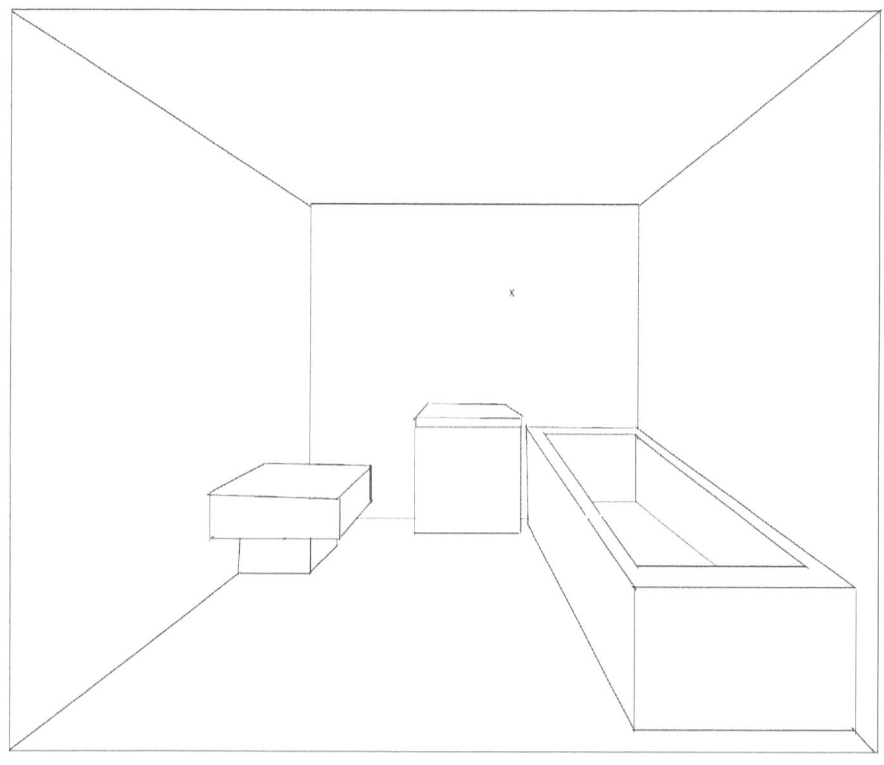

Tidy the drawing -
remove hidden
lines.

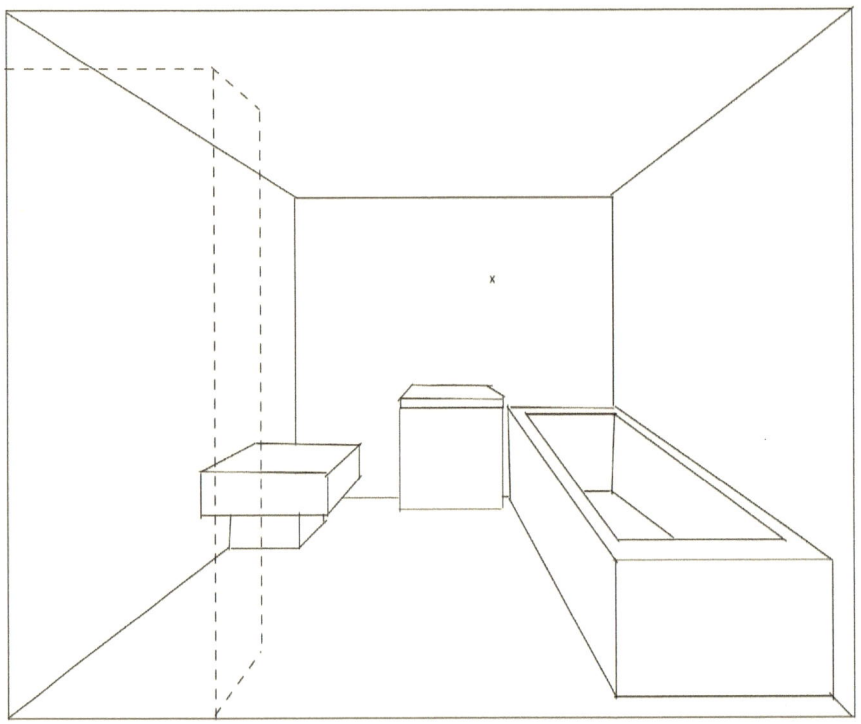

Add the shower -
ghosted form is the
best depiction

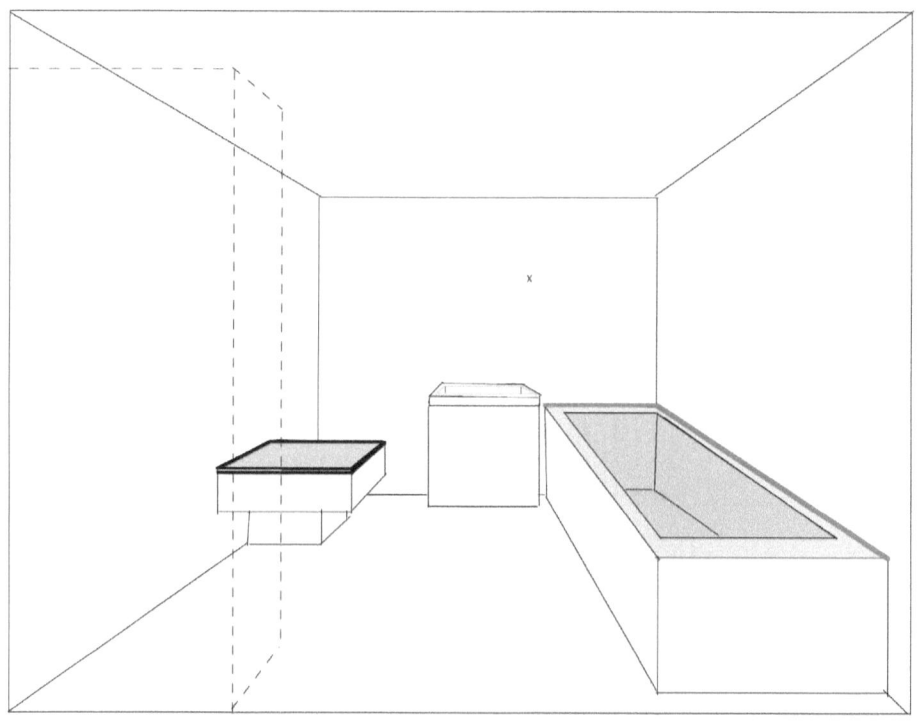

Continue with the
detail - shading
works well to
enhance bathroom
fittings

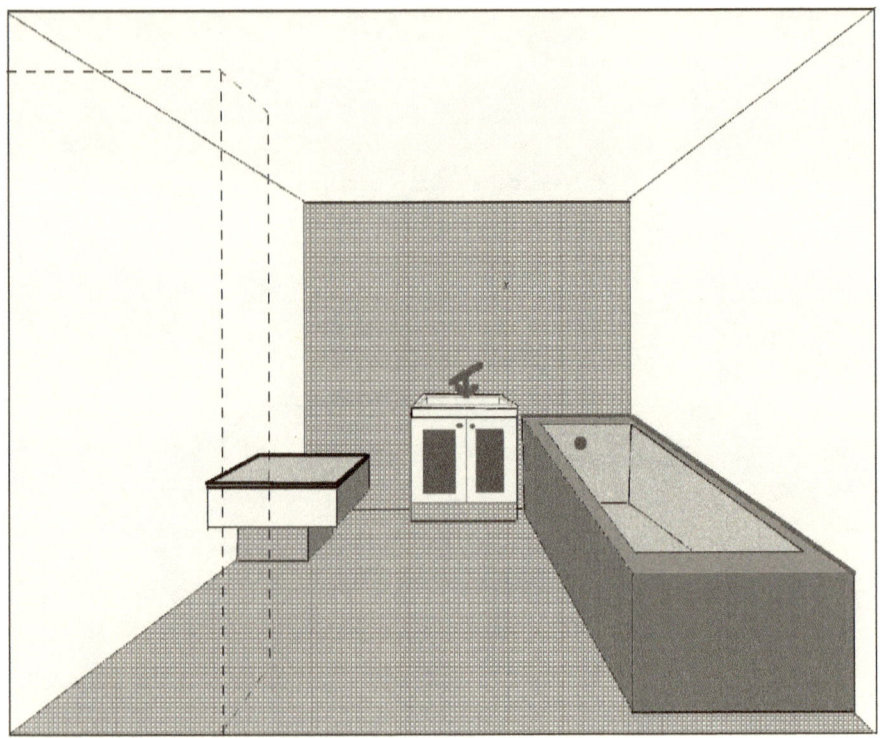

Complete the
drawing with some
subtle rendering
adding further
detail if you wish

The Perspective Ruler©

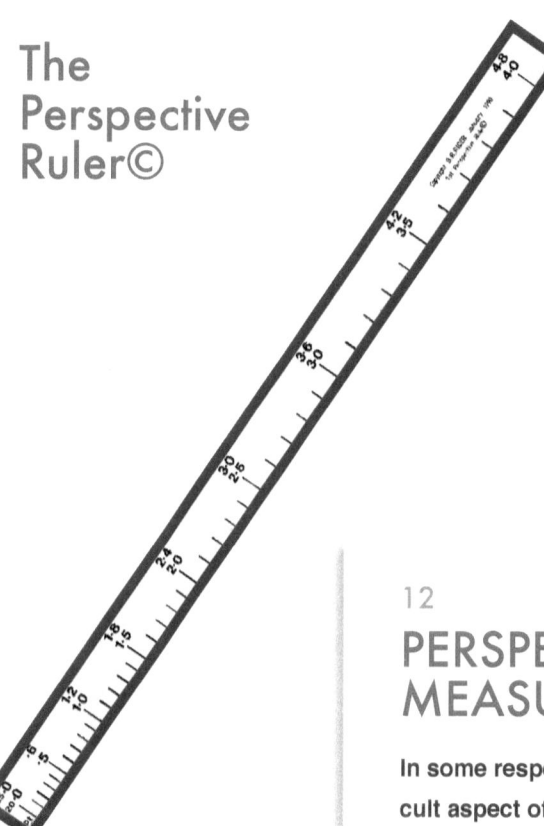

12

PERSPECTIVE MEASUREMENTS

In some respects this is the most diffi-cult aspect of perspective, but mainly 1 point and 2 point perspectives. The method is more or less the same for both so we shall just elaborate on the basic principles.

One of the things that our Designers found was that they could not teach their delegates how to judge the dimensions. We had developed the scale ruler as shown earlier. This was simple, effective and allowed the delegates to relax and get on with the more important drawing skills. In fact, it isn't really necessary but it is a big help in distance learning and for speed of the drawing. We shall show over the next few pages how to interpret the return measurements in a variety of different ways.

For simplicity for at least the first few drawings we strongly recommend using the Perspective Ruler©. All you have to do is to plot the measurements - cumulatively. Don't use it like an ordinary ruler measuring 600mm then another 600mm then say 500mm you must measure 600mm then 1200mm then 1700mm which you can do without moving the ruler.

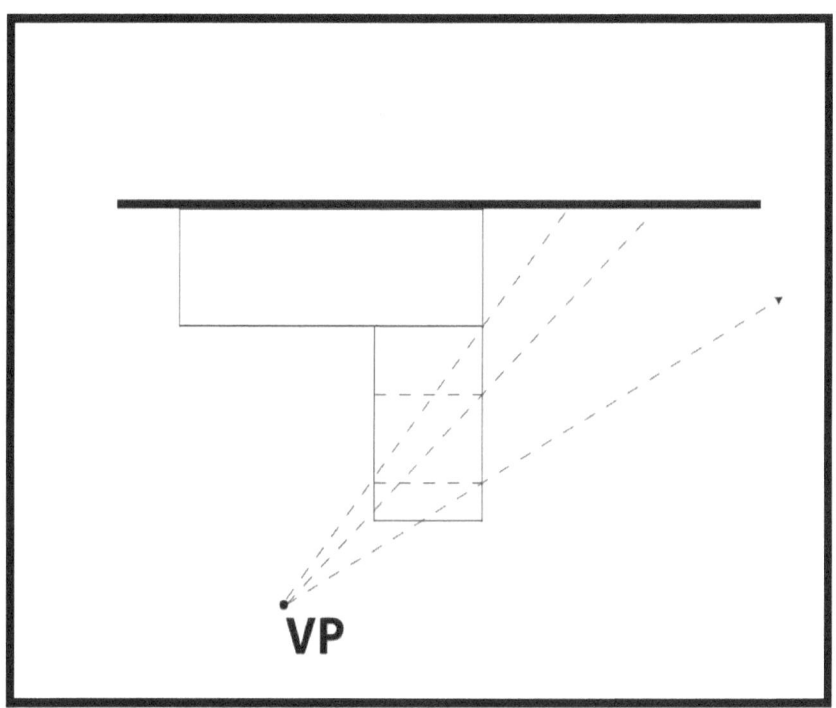

VP

PERSPECTIVE MEASUREMENTS THE FORMAL METHOD

This is the proper method to achieve accurate and consistent return measurements. Please note the VP shown is in fact the viewing point although it is in effect, an additional vanishing point. If you start with your original scale plan you should then transfer the return wall to your perspective drawing (we have shown it here as a group of kitchen units. You then choose your VP - it is not critical except the view that it provides. The VP should be as far away as possible on your drawing board or even off the board. Using the VP just like a vanishing point you line up the VP with the measurements of the individual units and project them to the wall shown as a solid line. For a more compact image you would project the floor line in perspective and then transfer the measurements to this line instead of the back wall line - the choice is yours. You then draw in perspective from your drawing vanishing points.

Point to note

Locate the viewing point as far away as practical - the further away the more condensed the return measurements

Always start with the ends of the wall - this then sets your final scale from your original scale plan

It is possible to transfer the return wall measurements directly on your perspective but to begin with use your scale plan and then transfer only the measuring points

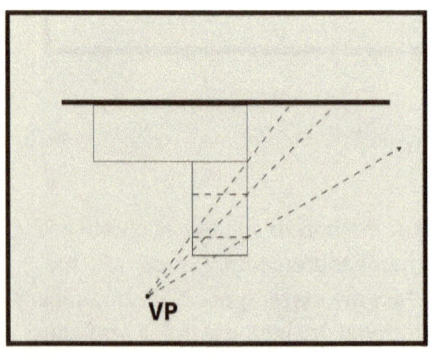

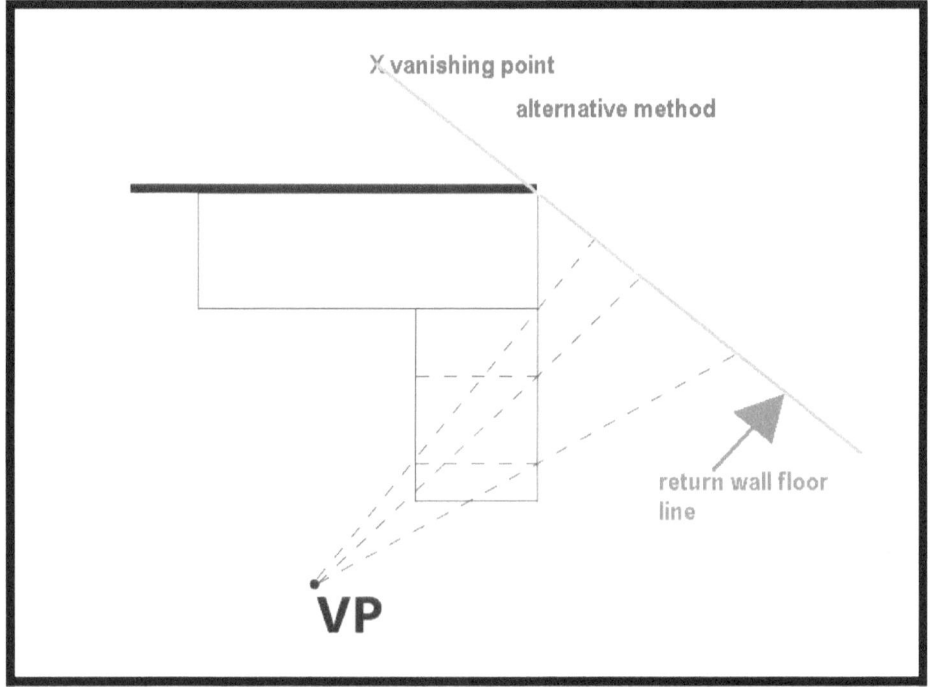

X vanishing point

alternative method

return wall floor
line

VP

Alternative method using a perspective return wall

Using the same initial steps project the return wall floor line from your chosen vanishing point, Then from your chosen viewing point transfer the individual unit divisions to the return wall line rather than the floor line. This then provides a slightly more compact drawing especially if the room is larger than average. Try it a few times until you get the hang of it. Use a simple scale plan with method one and then practice with the alternative method. Once you get the hang of the return wall you will, in fact, either use the copied perspective ruler or simply judge the room. As you can automatically find the end of the room or the section of the room you wish to draw judging the intermediate steps is quite a simple progression so all you really need is the end of the room and a few intermediate measurements and judge the rest - you will soon get the hang of it.

13

2 POINT PERSPECTIVE

The 2 point is more demanding and time consuming but generally gives the best balanced view in wide projects such as a kitchen. You can also expand this into a multipoint perspective but for most projects this is probably not necessary.

So on to the 2 point. For larger rooms you may find this useful but it should become obvious for each project. You simply use your judgment to get the best view for your project. Except for the fact you have two vanishing points and you draw from the vanishing point to one or the other walls depending upon whether you are projecting in or out, the steps are virtually the same as 1 point.

But be careful - many of the examples shown for 2 point are for buildings - not interiors. If you are drawing buildings this is the correct format but it is not suitable for interiors except possibly very large open internal spaces.

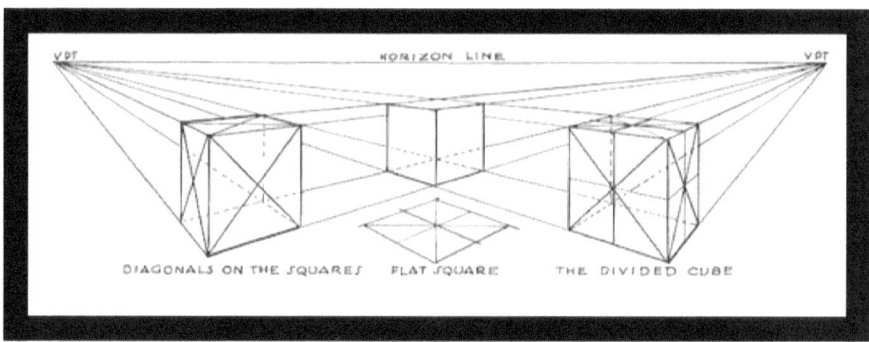

This is the method to use for interiors

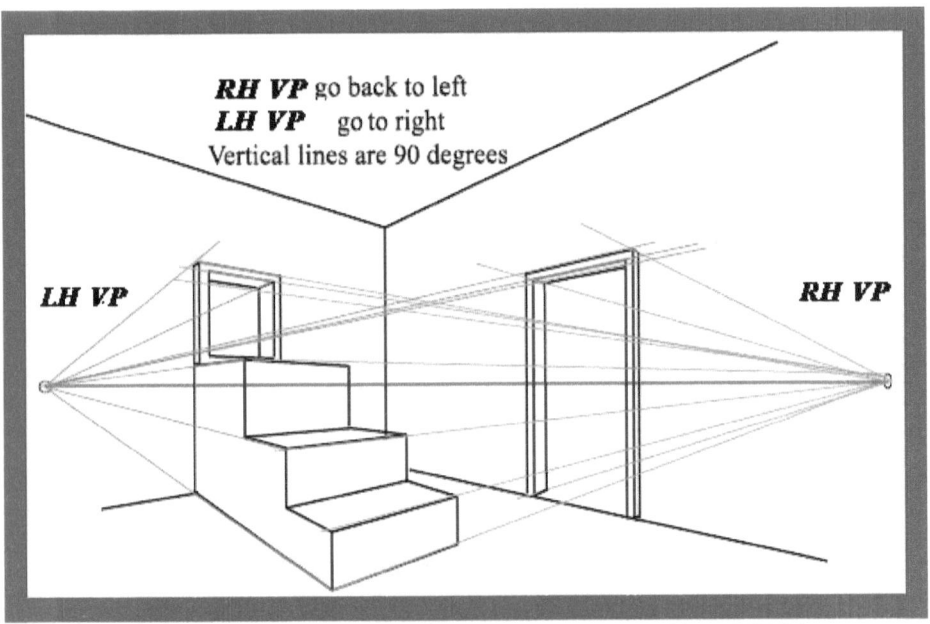

RH VP go back to left
LH VP   go to right
Vertical lines are 90 degrees

LH V.P   RH VP

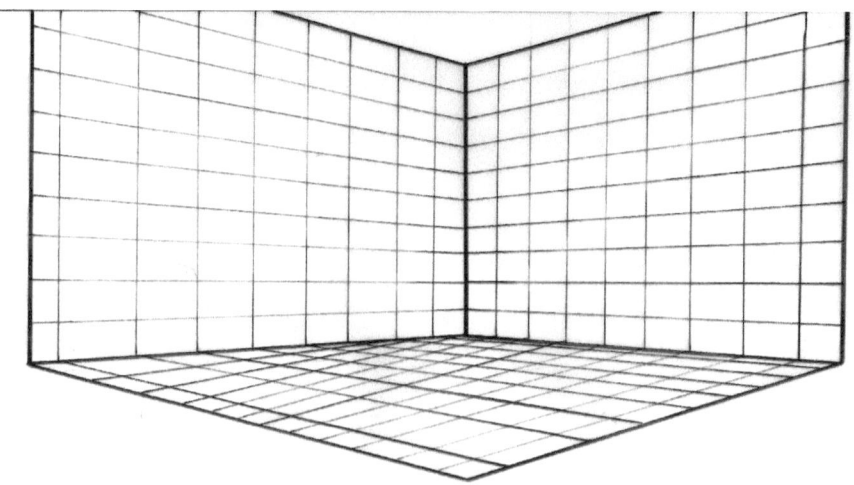

As before you can use a grid or construct a grid but it is very boring and quite tedious and does not provide the best view for all presentations. The time factor is actually better with the proper method each time. The drawing below shows a new interior start. Ignore the third point on the lower corner this is a measuring point.

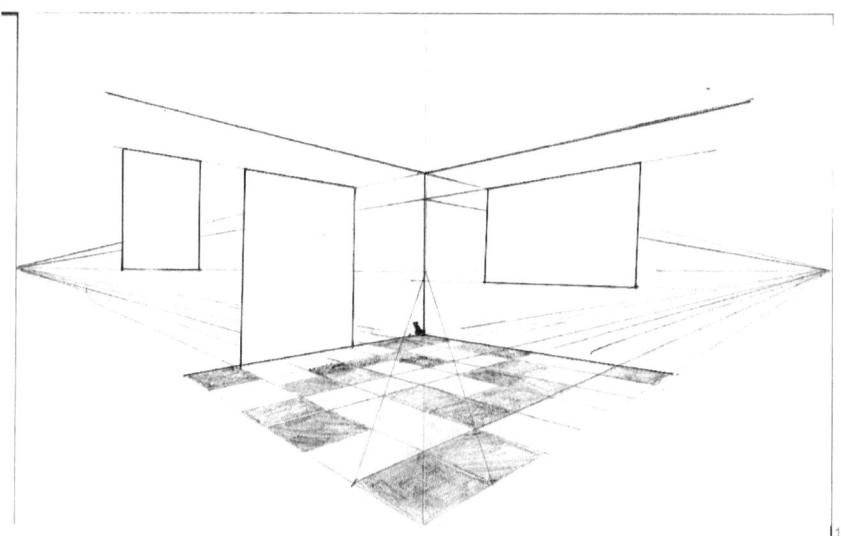

As before start with
the corner of the
room in scale and
refer to your scale
plan.

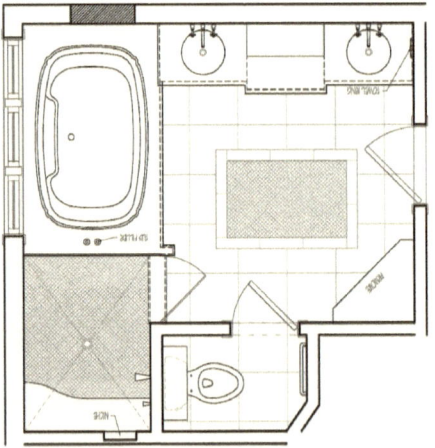

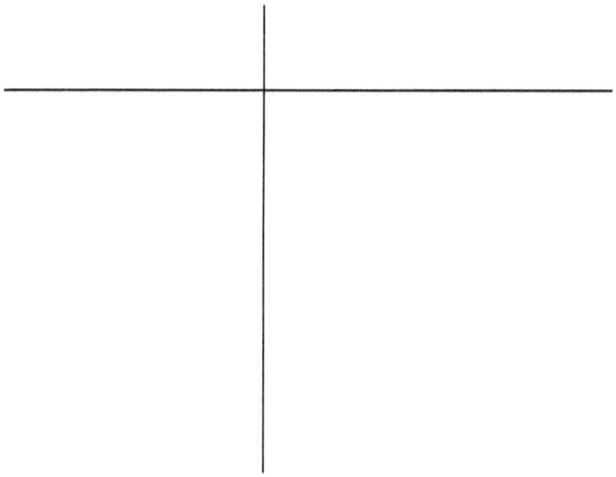

Now choose your
horizon line -
default is 1600mm

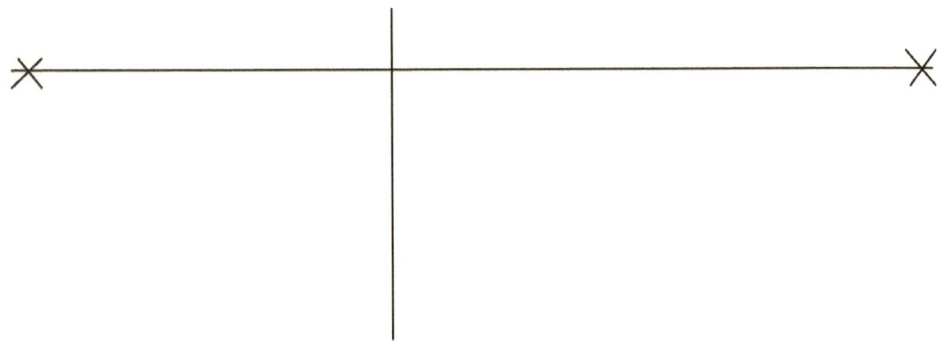

Now choose your
vanishing points -
as far as the board
allows

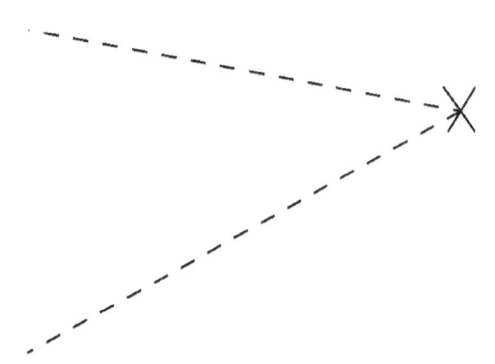

Next line up the VP
to project the walls

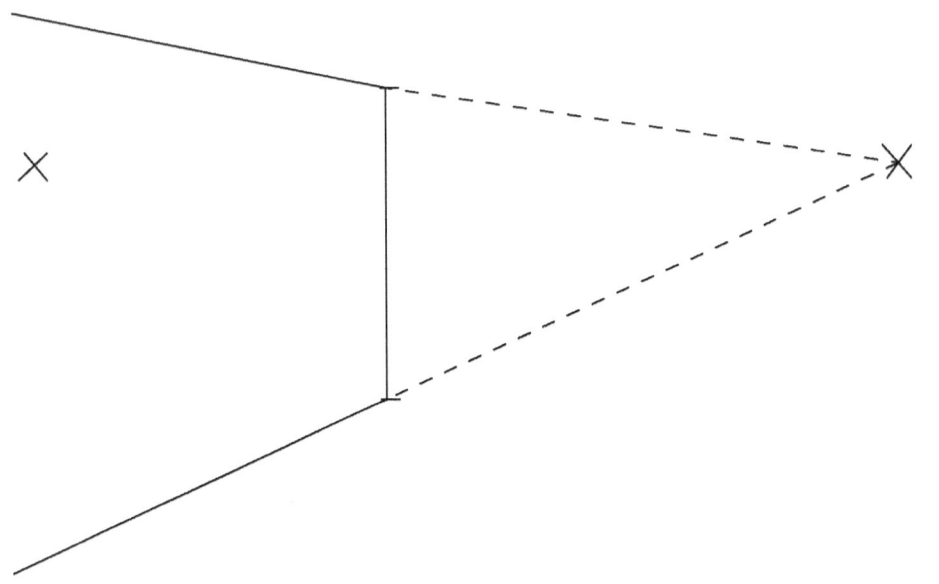

Continue with
projecting the walls

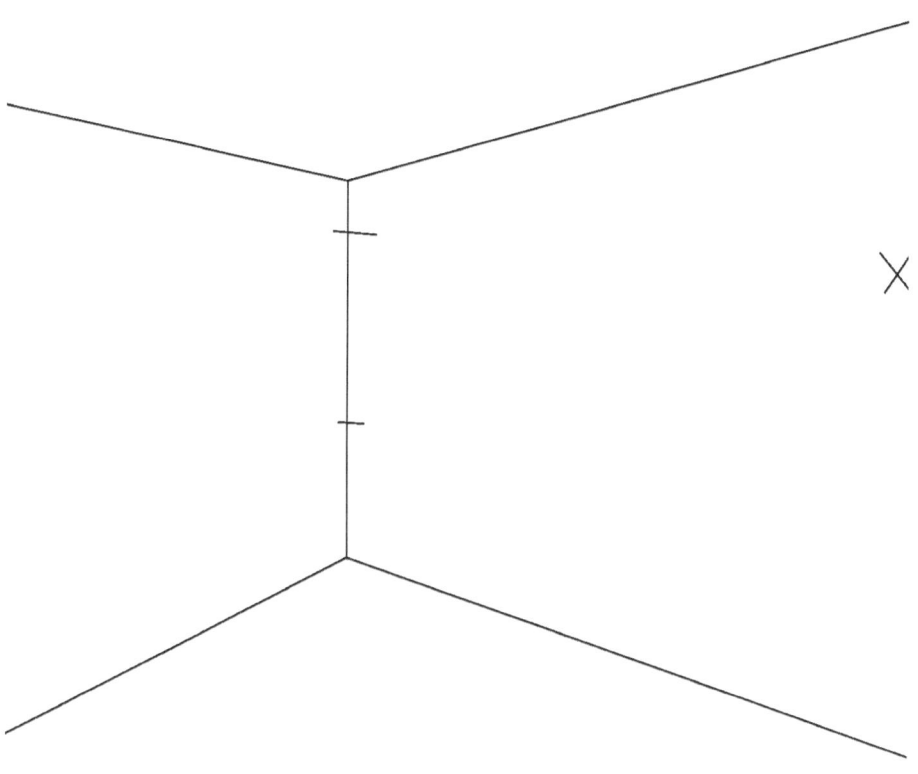

X

We have now
completed the walls
but not found the
ends.

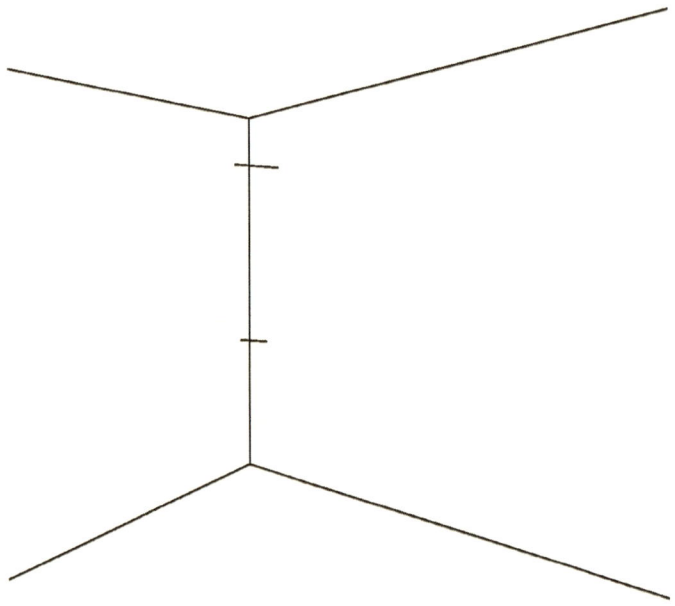

**Set up the content
outline**

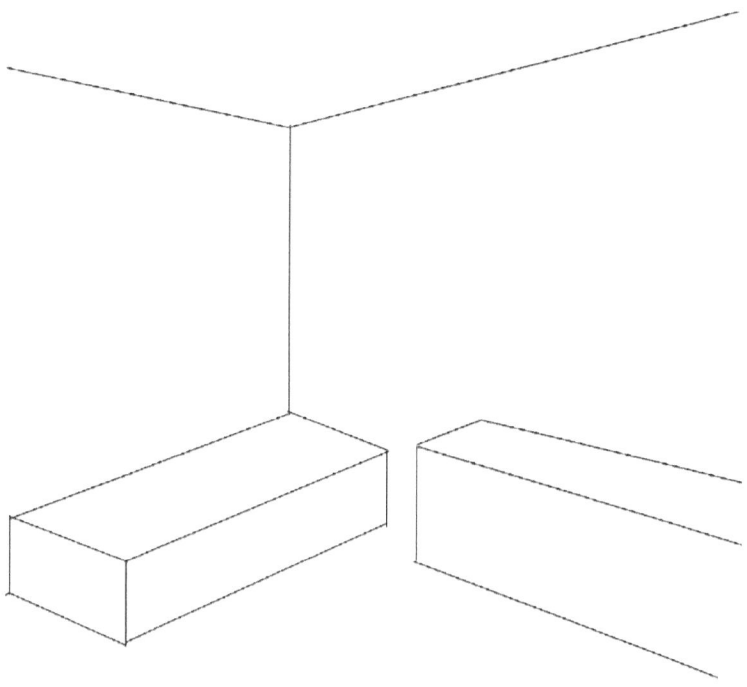

Continue with the
content outlines

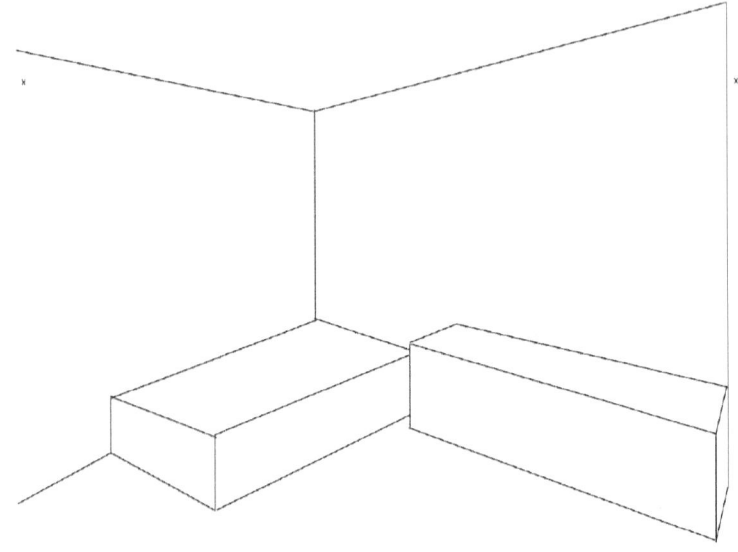

Continue the
content outline and
detail

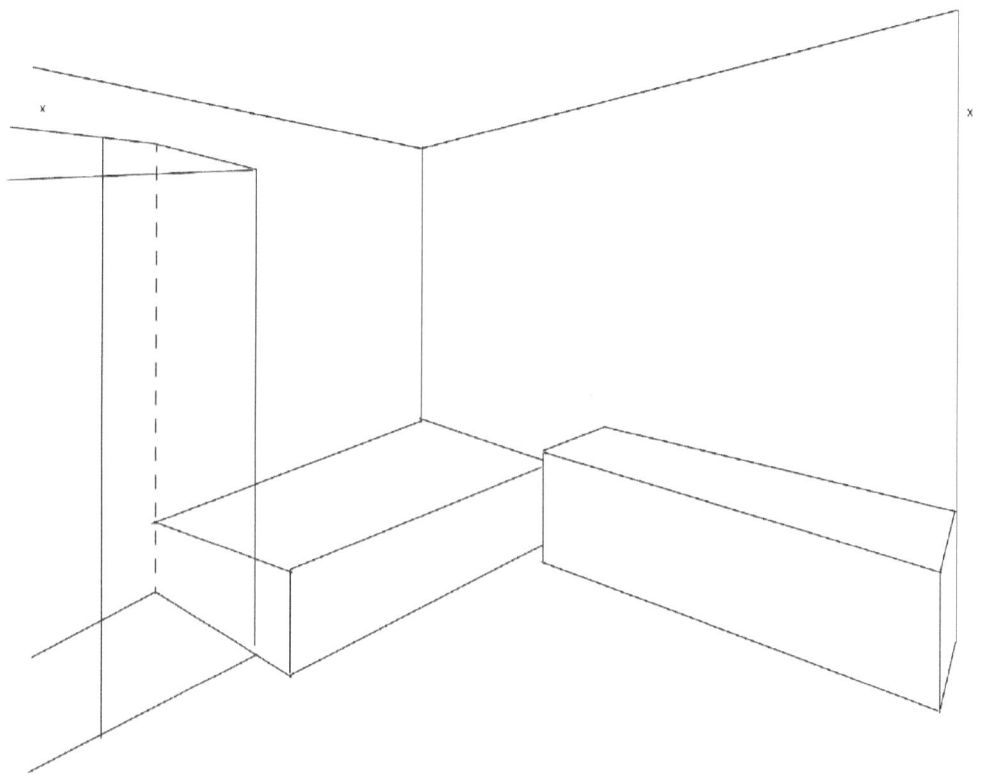

Now construct the
tall structure to the
left - this is a
shower enclosure

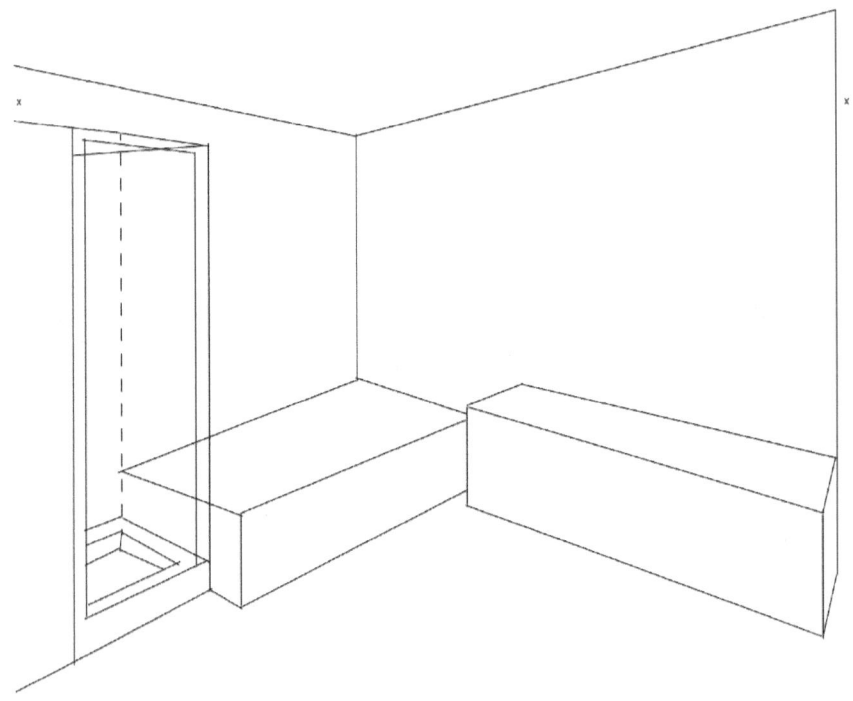

Continue detailing
the shower
enclosure

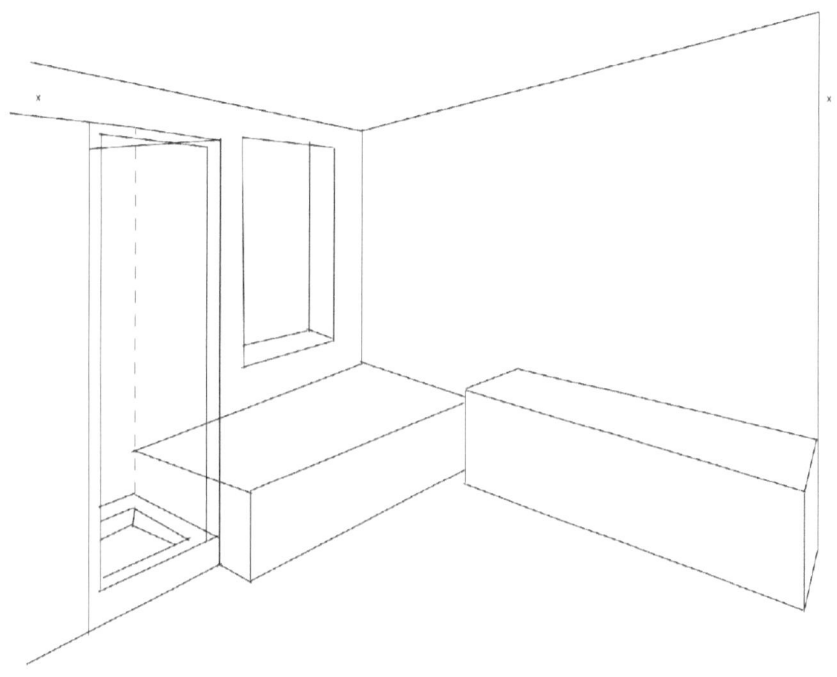

Continue with room
and content
detailing

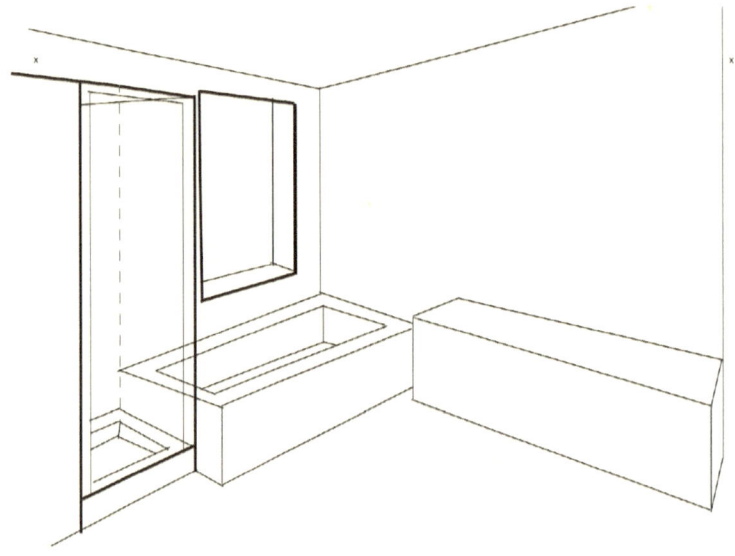

Continue with finer
and internal
detailing

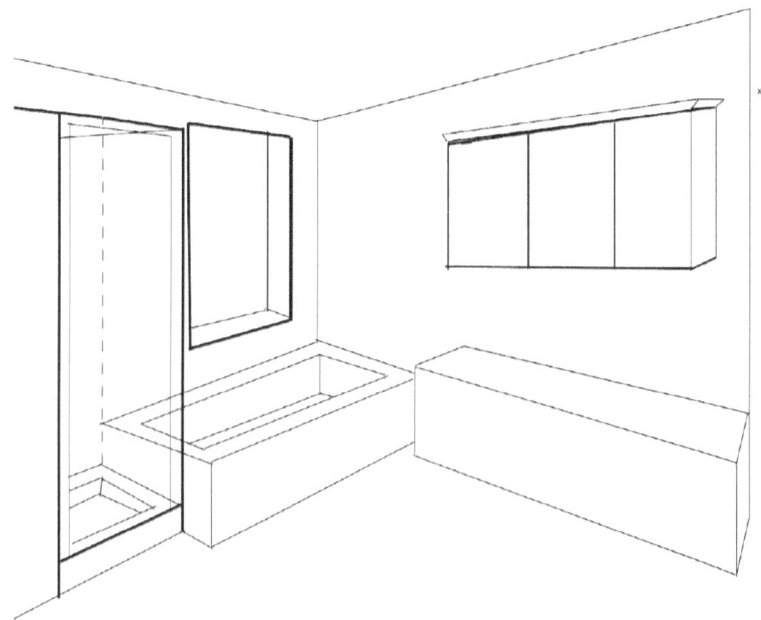

x

Next start adding
some wall
carcassing

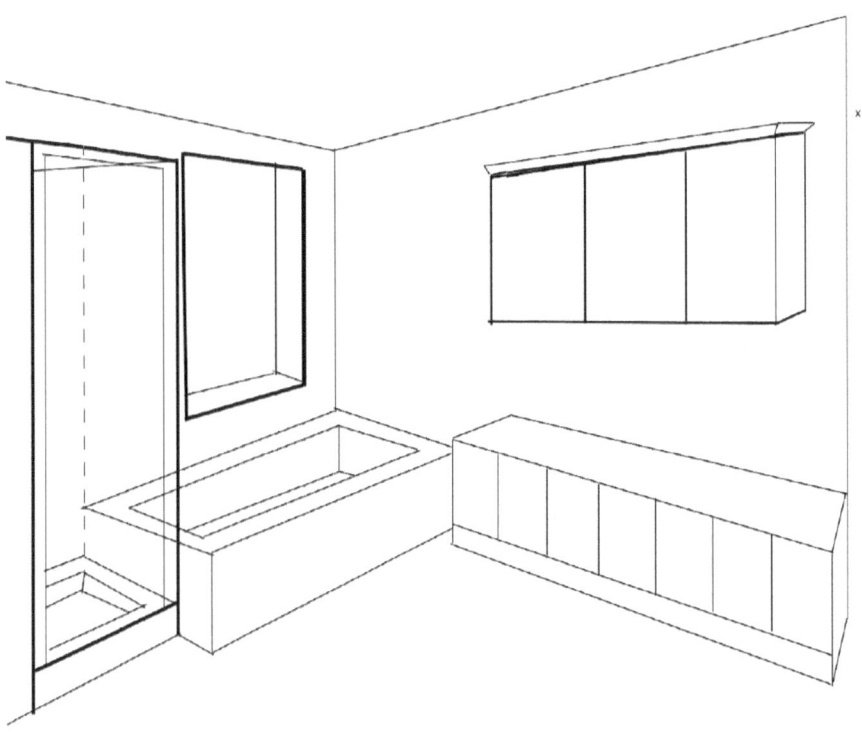

x

Complete the
carcassing qnd
door sizes using
your perspective
ruler

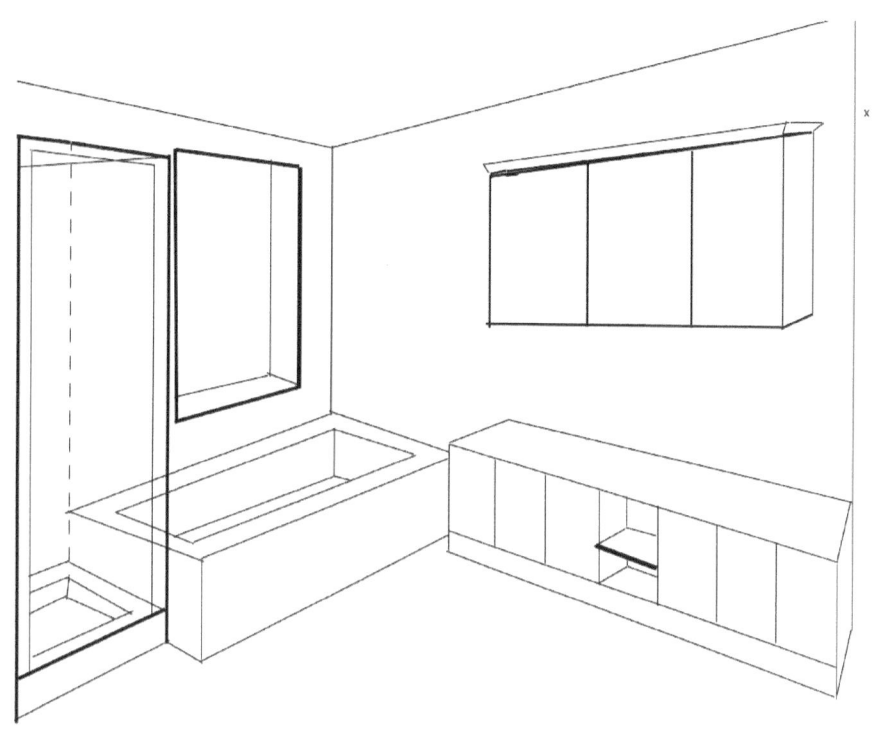

Finish detailing

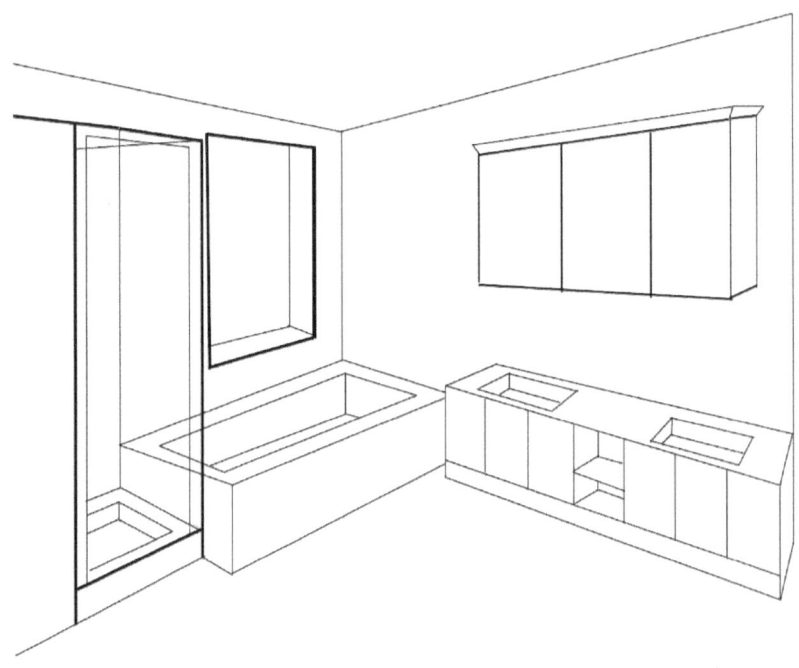

Detailing now quite
complete but you
can add worktop
thickness; plinth
inset etc: as
desired:

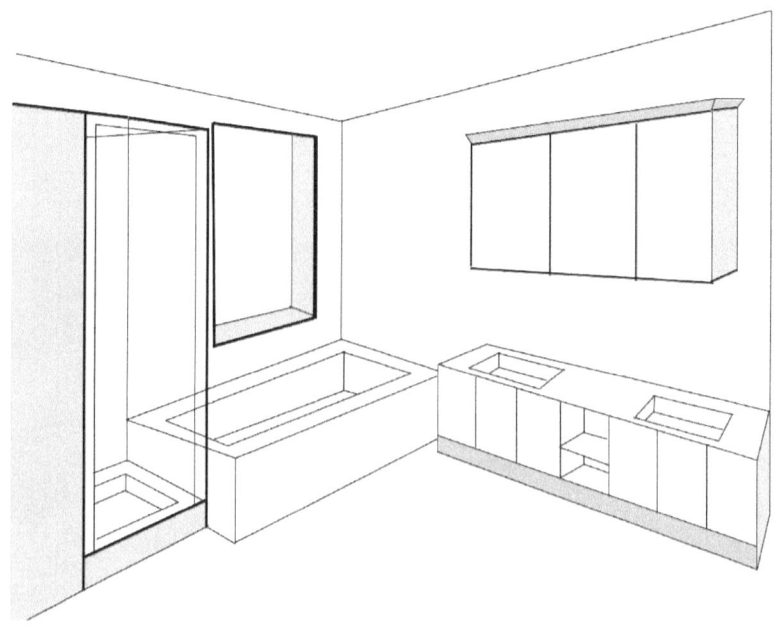

A splash of
rendering

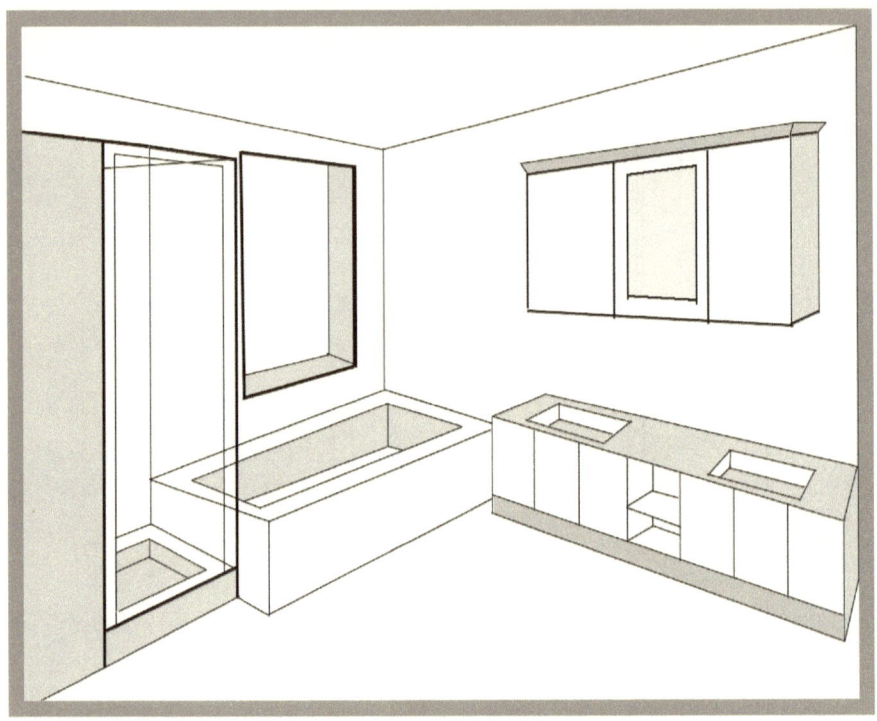

Final detail and
rendering as per
choice

ROOM
EXAMPLES

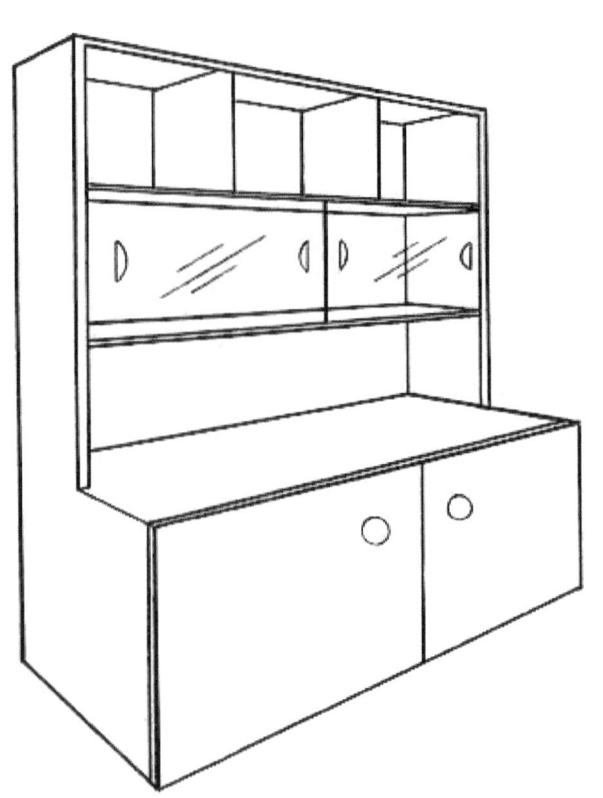

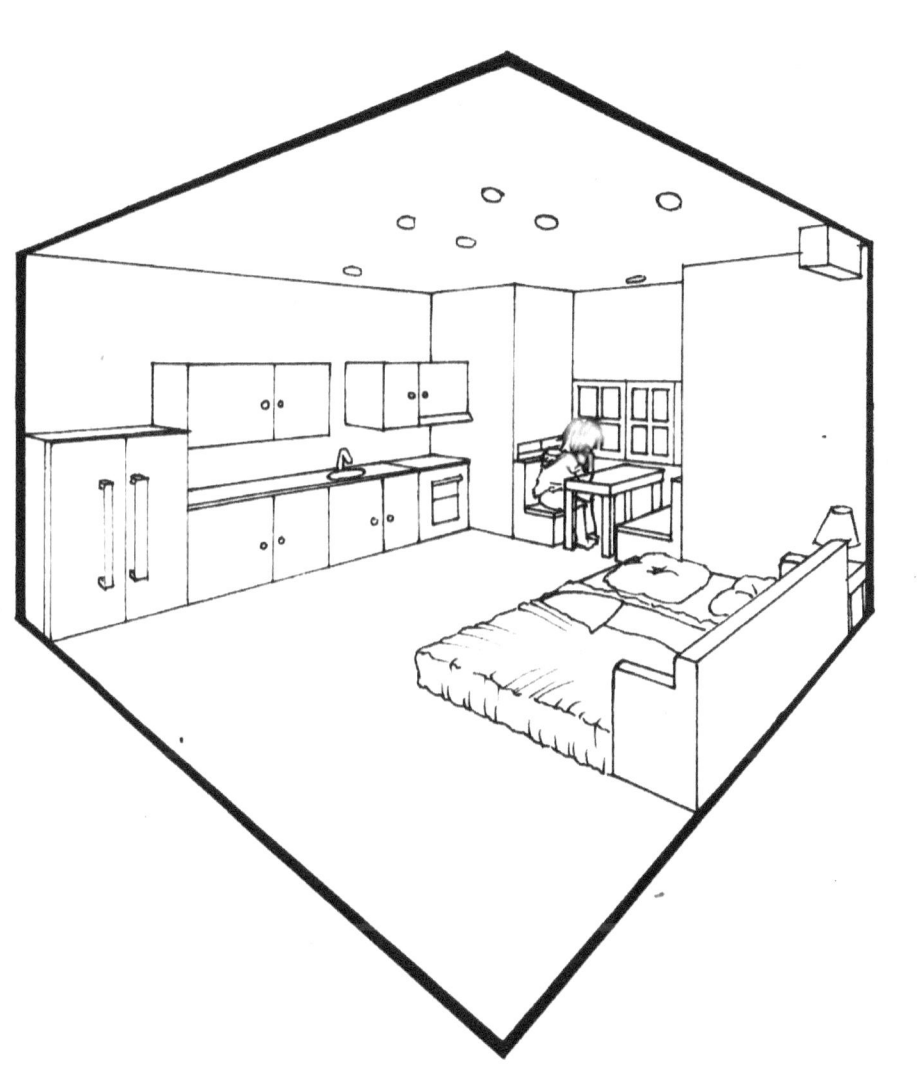

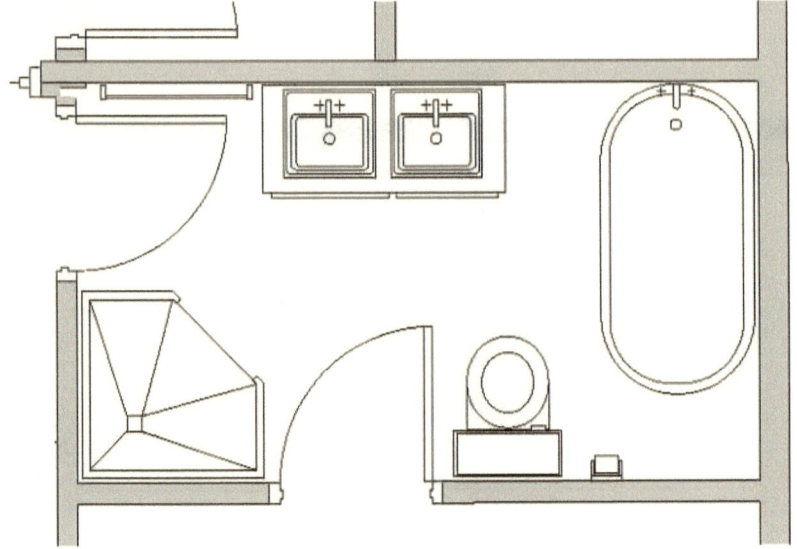

EXERCISE

Why not have a go? You can use this exercise for any method. In fact it might be a good idea to use it for all the methods just to familiarise yourself with all the different techniques: If you want to submit your drawings please go to our support site.

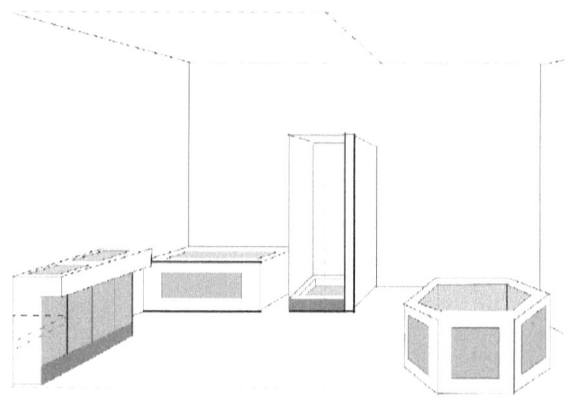

2 POINT BATHROOOM METHOD - MULTIPOINT

This is a form of multipoint perspective using the normal 2 point plus an interpretive 3rd point for median content. The main difference is that the back wall, rather than just the corner of the room, is in scale.

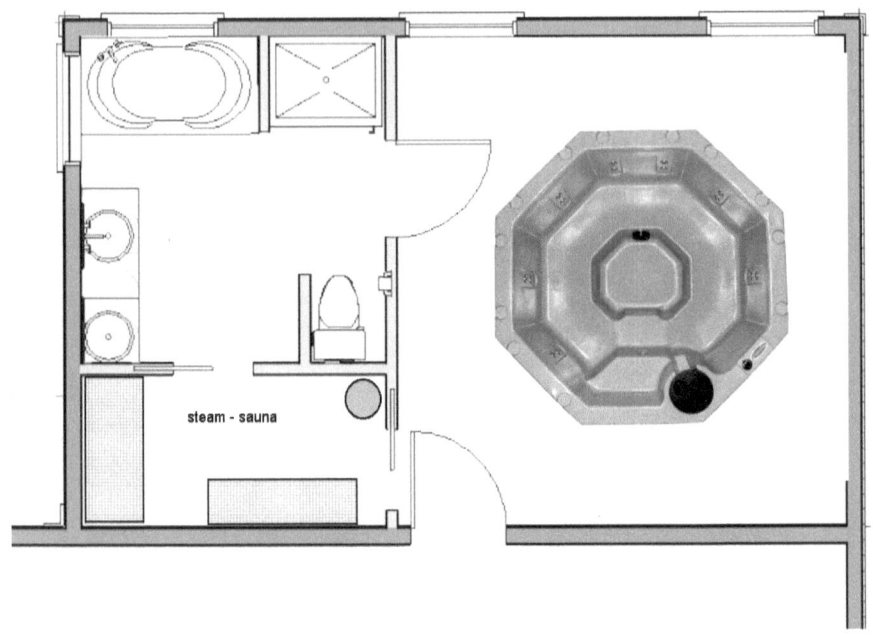

steam - sauna

As usual start with
your scale plan

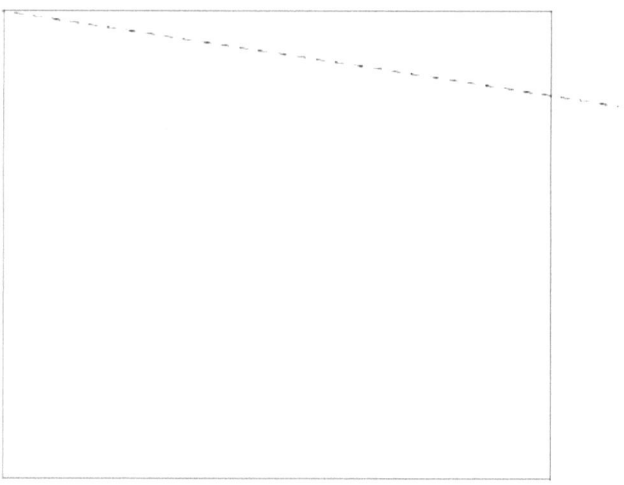

Start with the back
wall in scale

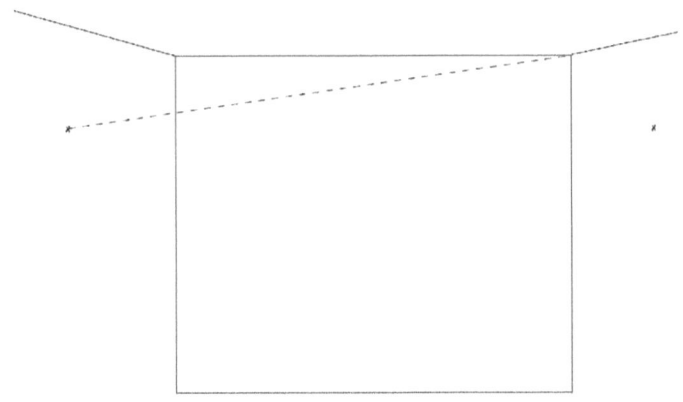

Locate your
vanishing points
and start projecting
the walls

Continue with your
walls - this is a big
room so you may
need to adjust your
view

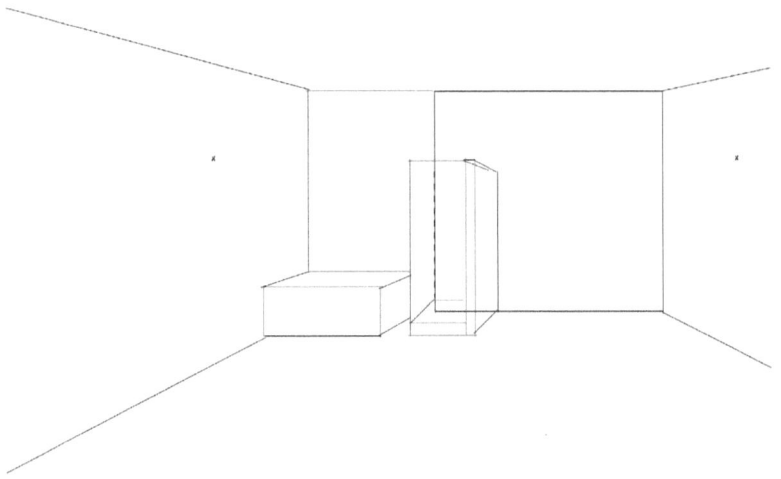

**start constructing
the basic shapes**

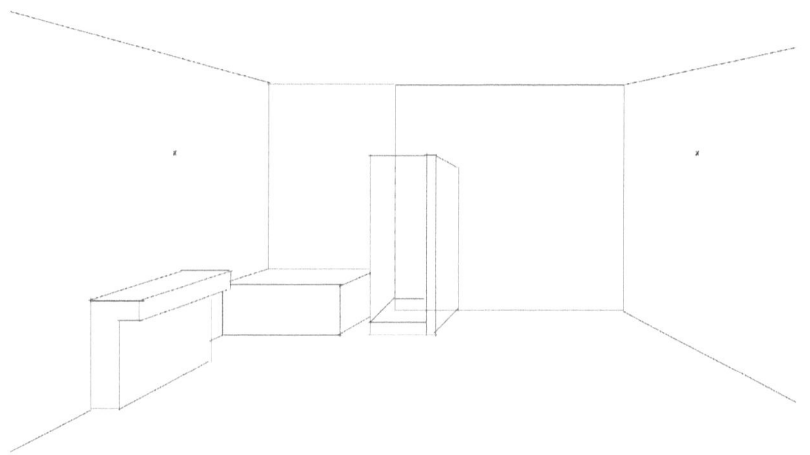

Continue with the
content

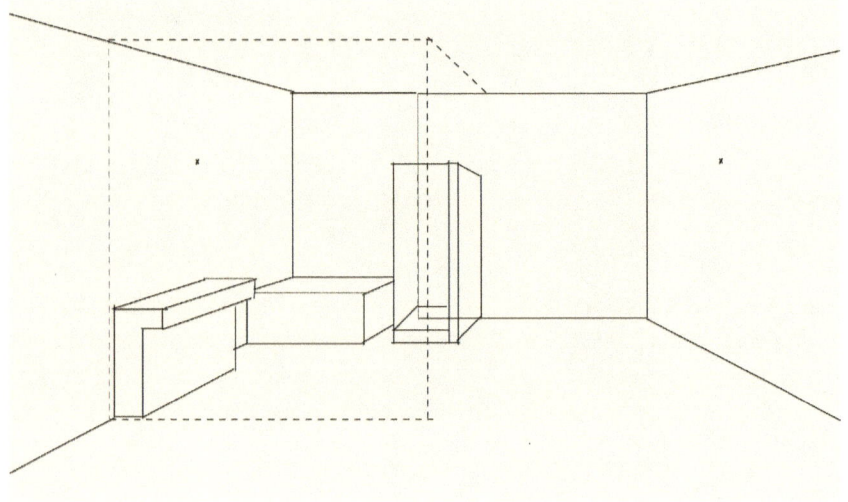

We are showing
the Steam room/
sauna in ghosted
(dotted) outline

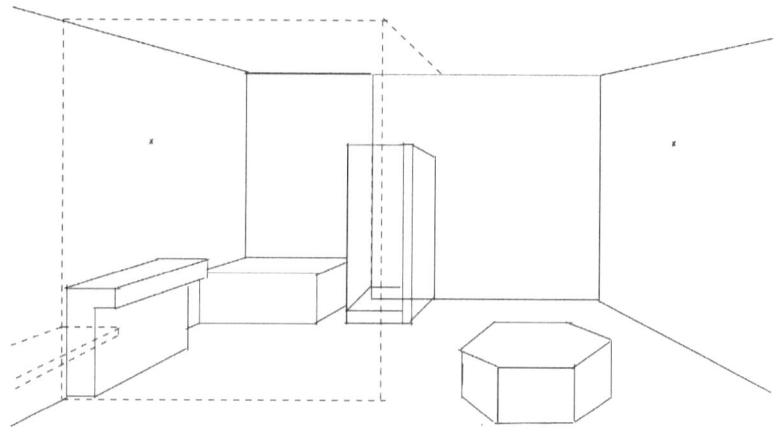

We are now
starting on the hot
tub - needs a bit of
tweeking to get it
right

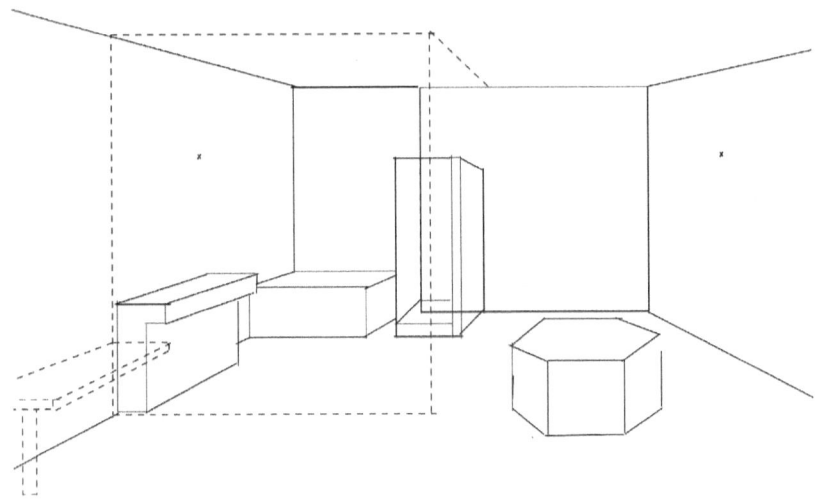

Continue with the
detail - notice the
bench in the Sauna

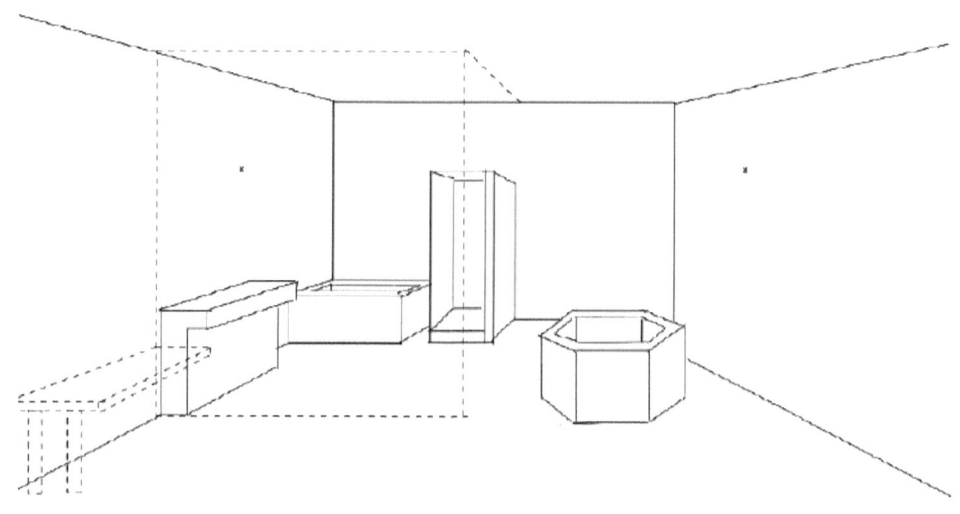

We are now
showing some
internal detail

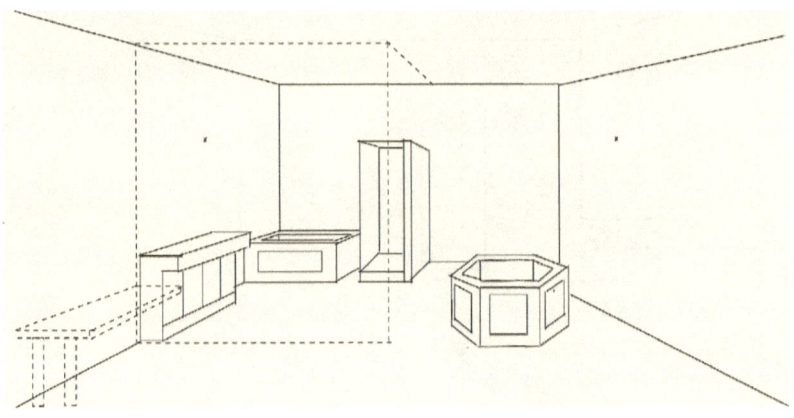

Building up the detail

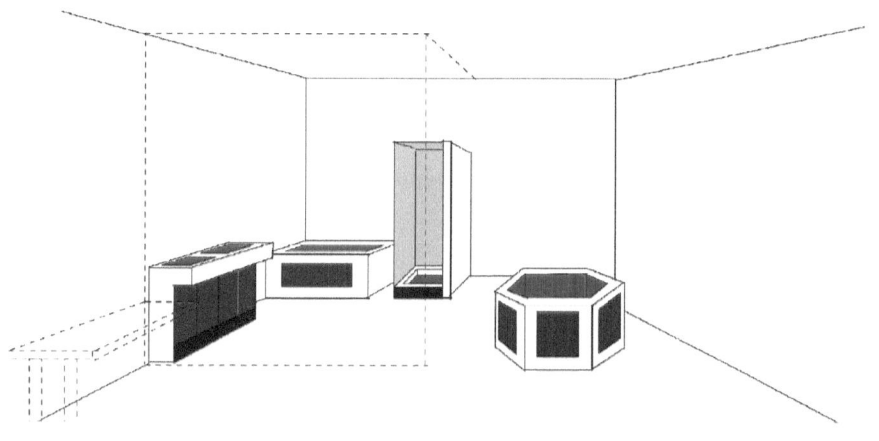

Starting to Render

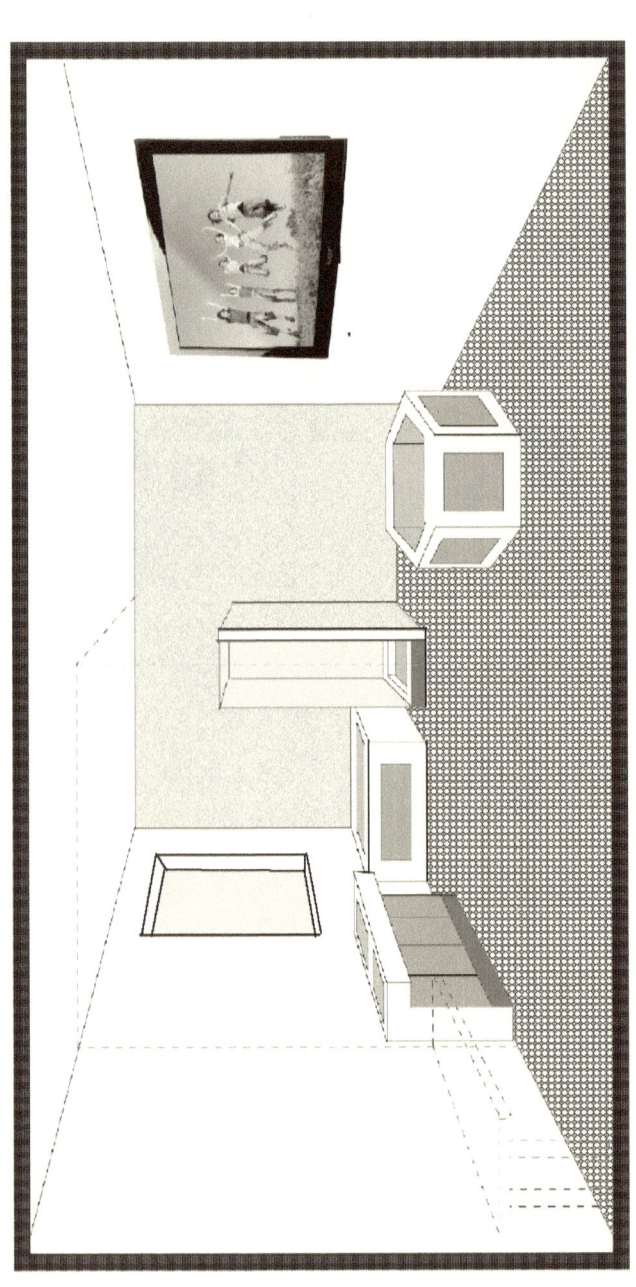

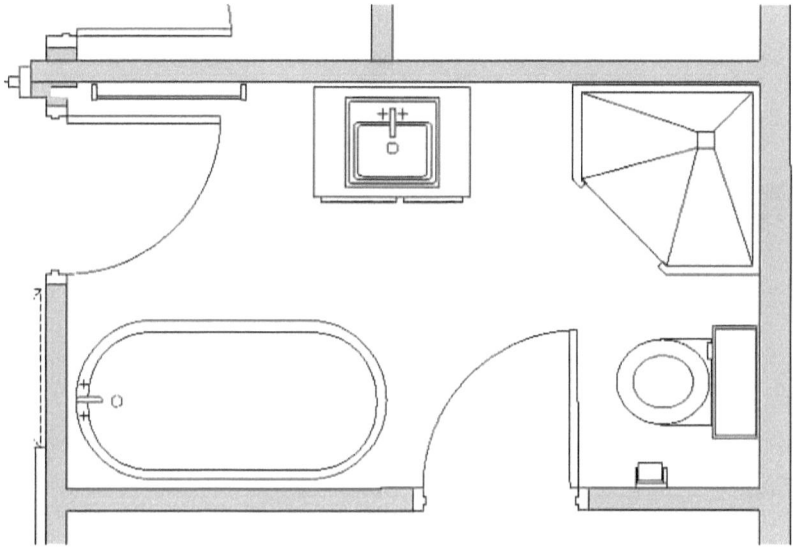

Another exercise to try your hand at. Particularly for the next section - Birds Eye

You can try it with a standard rectangular bath or have a go at the freestanding bath shown.

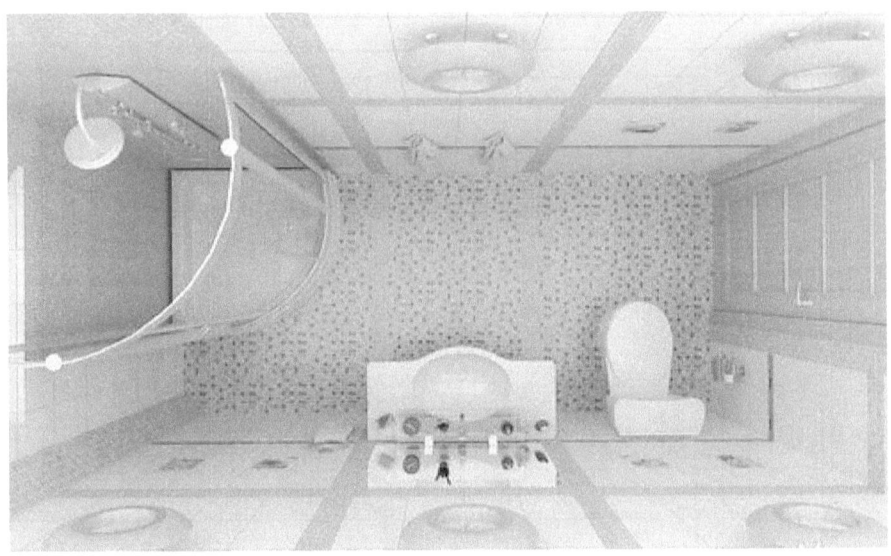

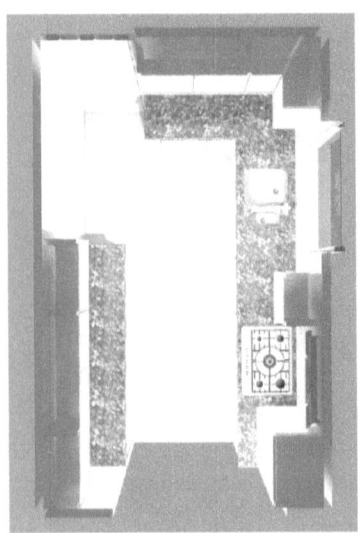

15

BIRD'S EYE PERSPECTIVE

This was always my favourite for kitchens as you can create the 3d drawing very quickly from your plan or a reduction thereof. The big advantage in presentation is that you can see the entire project even where it is an elaborate construction with Islands, Peninsula etc.

Birds Eyes are one of the simplest 3d drawings. All you need is your original scale plan and, using tracing paper, simply select your vanishing point somewhere on the floor to project the walls units etc. in birds eye.

This is especially useful for showing really complex shapes and the beauty is you don't need to worry about perspective measurements just use an ordinary scale rule and measure along the vertical lines you are drawing. Works fine.

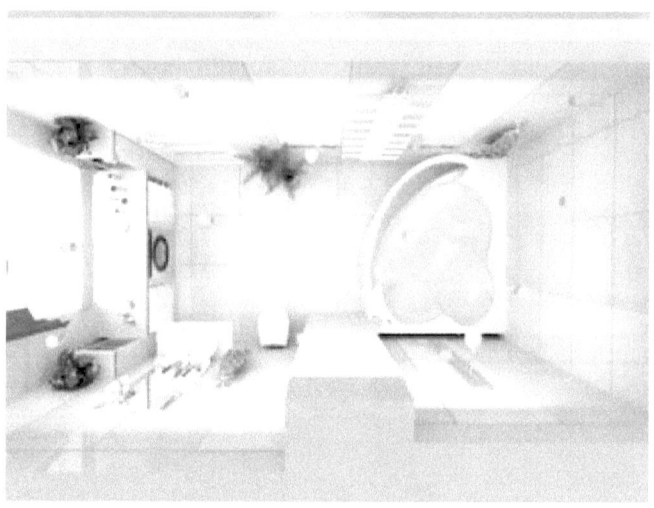

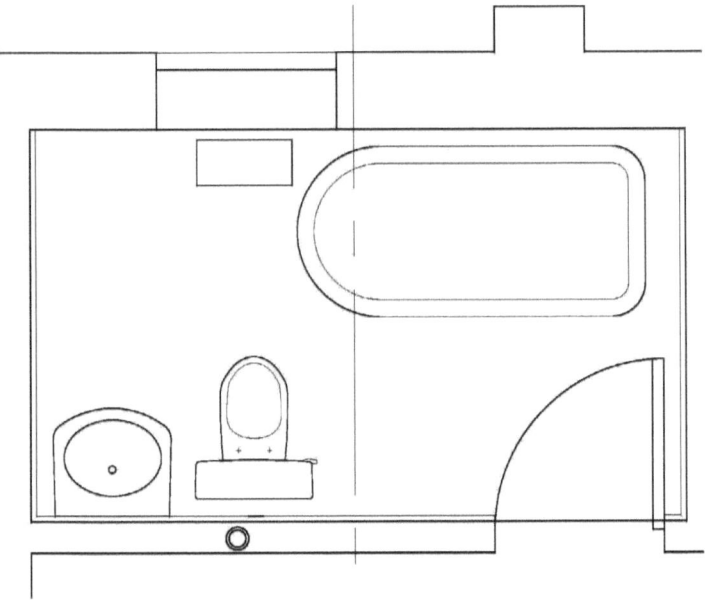

BIRD'S EYE TRANSFORMATION

We will try to transform this bathroom plan into a bird's eye. To keep the time at a minimum we will start with a rectangular bath. You can then try with a freestanding bath:

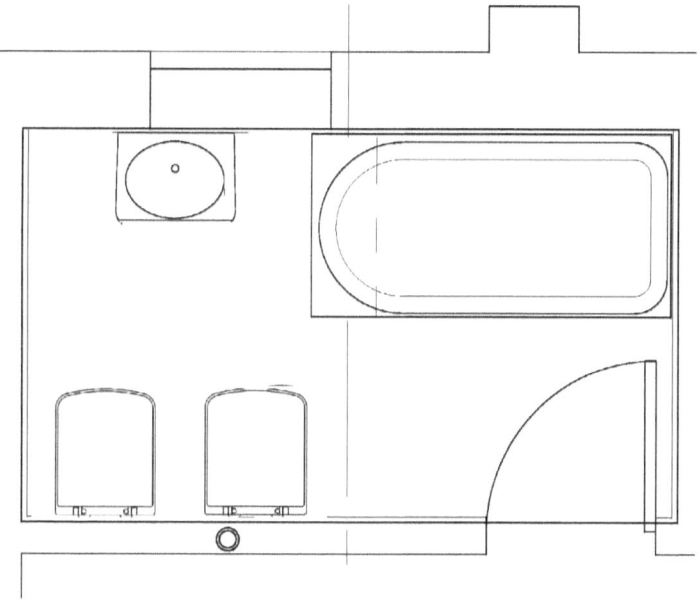

So this is the layout
we are working to
on the first exercise

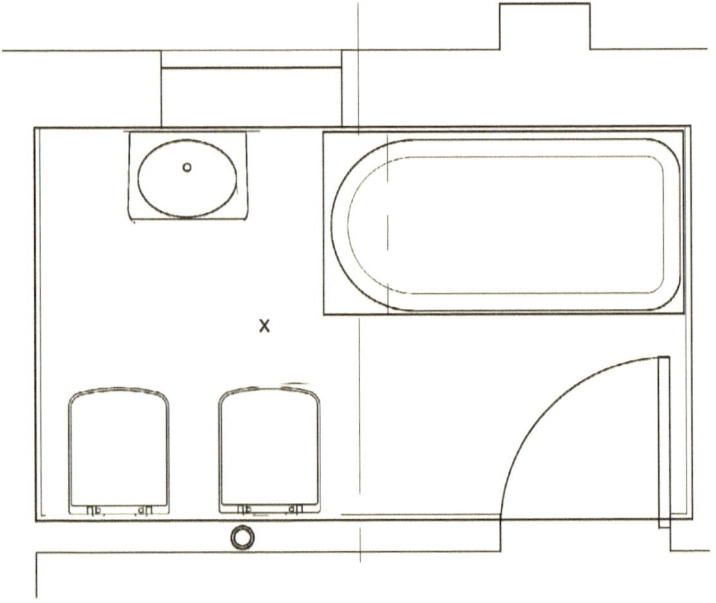

Locate your
vanishing point as
desired

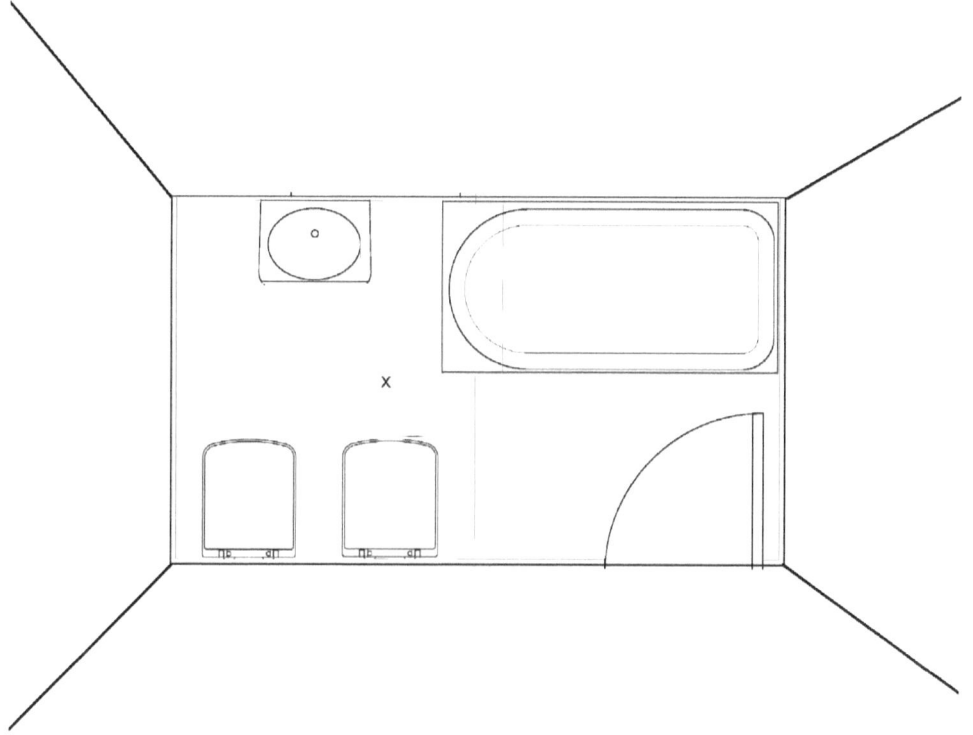

Strip the plan down
and project the
walls

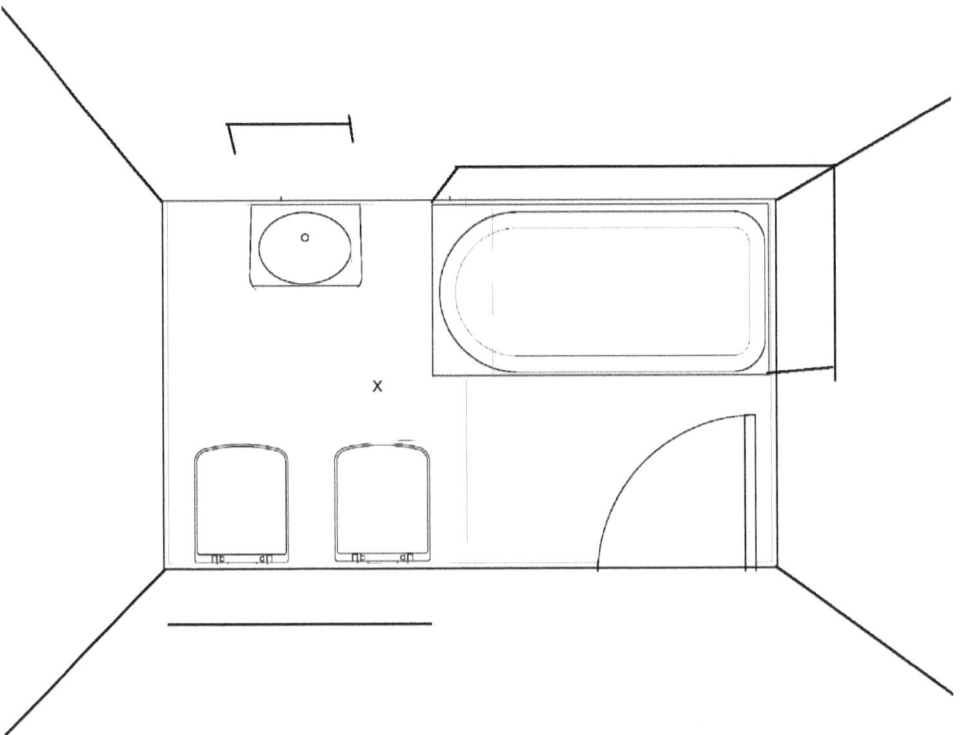

Start profiling the
fitments

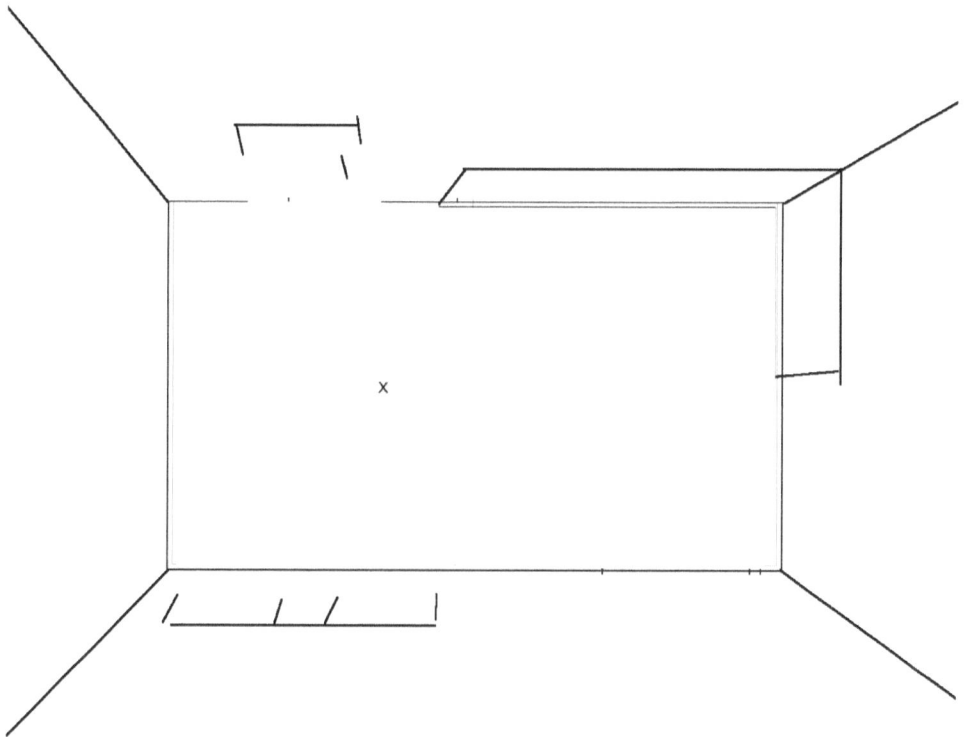

Finish profiling and
clear the rest of the
plan

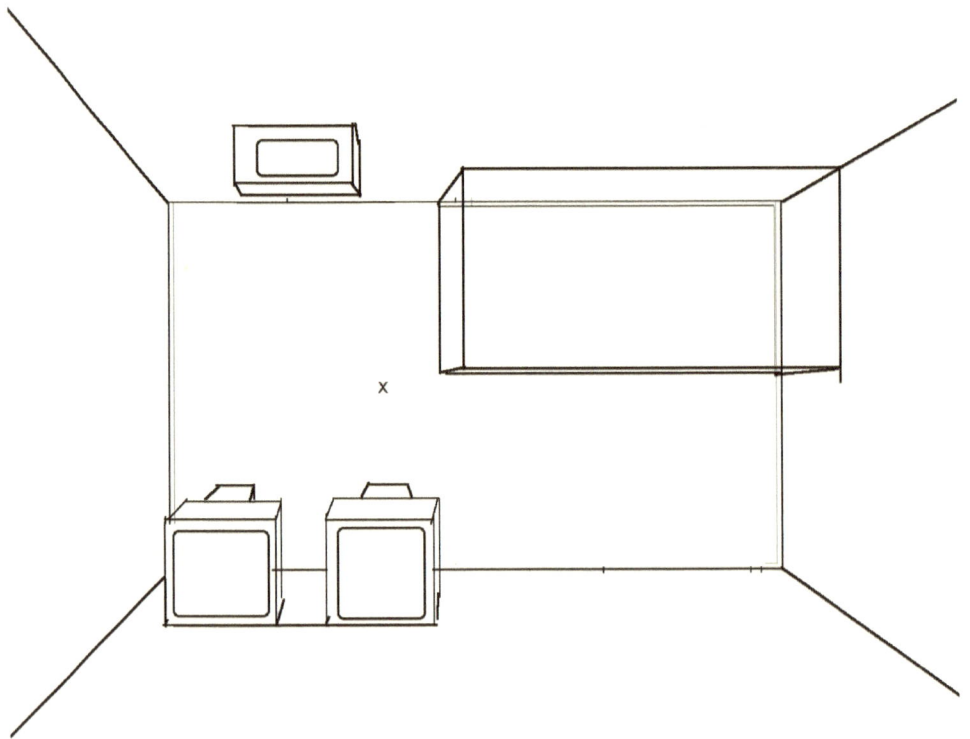

x

Now complete the
fitments outlines

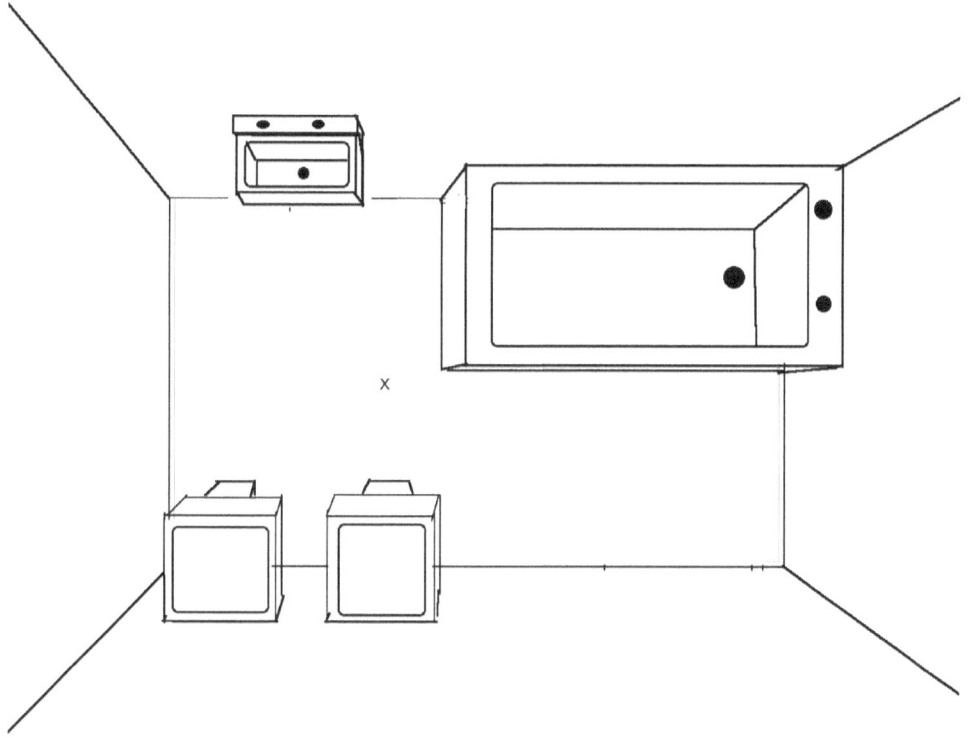

x

Complete detail
including interiors

172

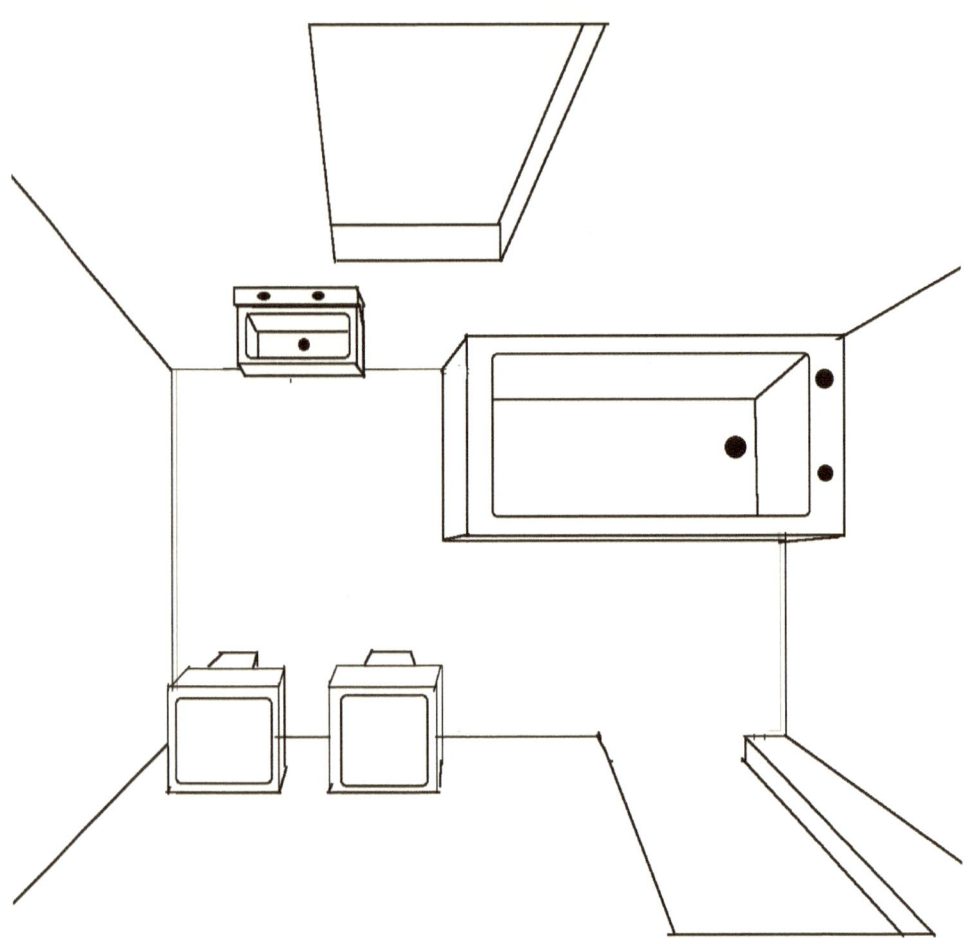

COMPLETE THE
ARCHITECTURAL
FEATURES

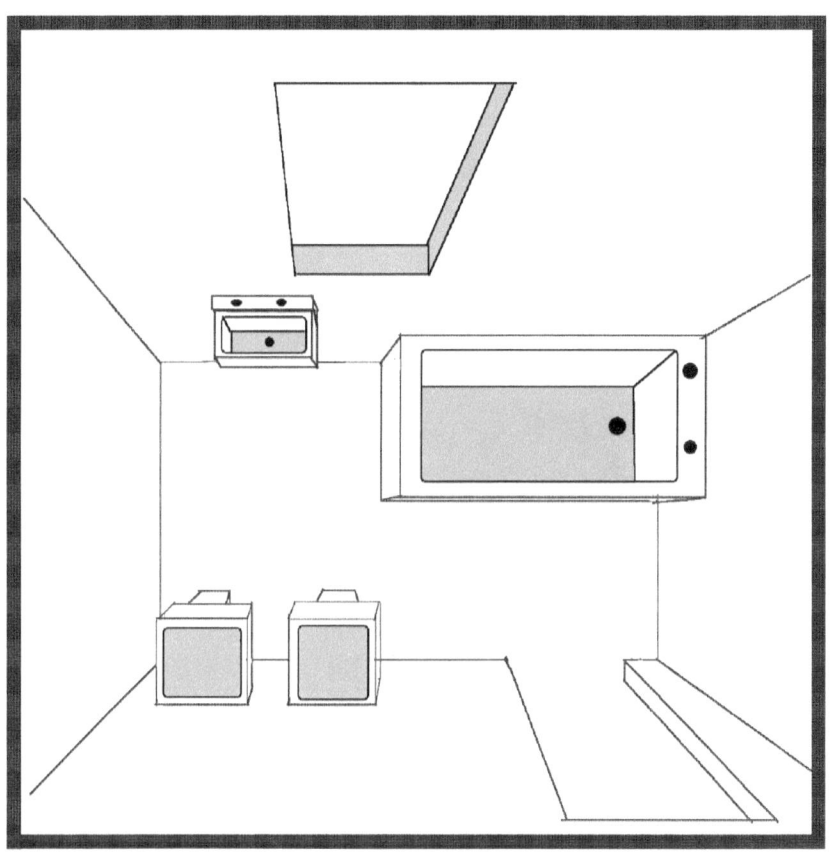

Complete and
render

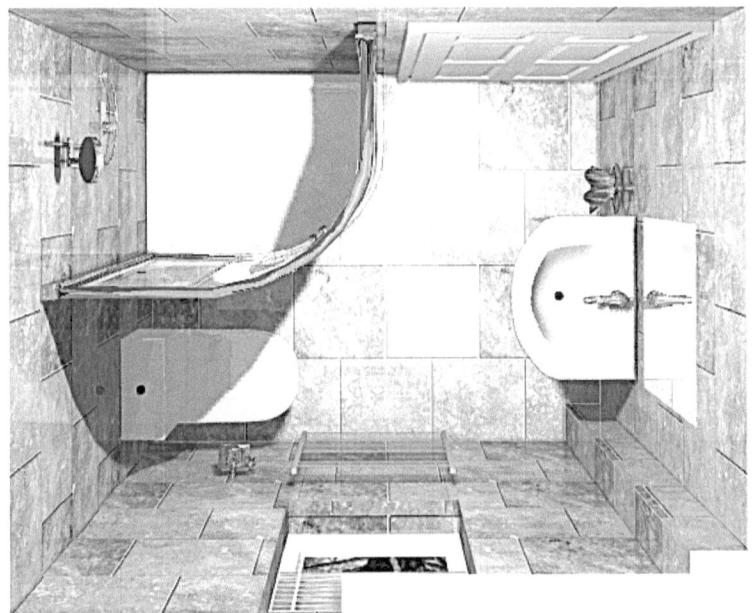

16

BIRD'S EYE
ESSENTIALS

Bird`s eye perspective offers the opportunity to draw the perspective directly from your scale plan: You also do not need to use any formal scale for the verticals but a 1:50 scale is perfectly useable

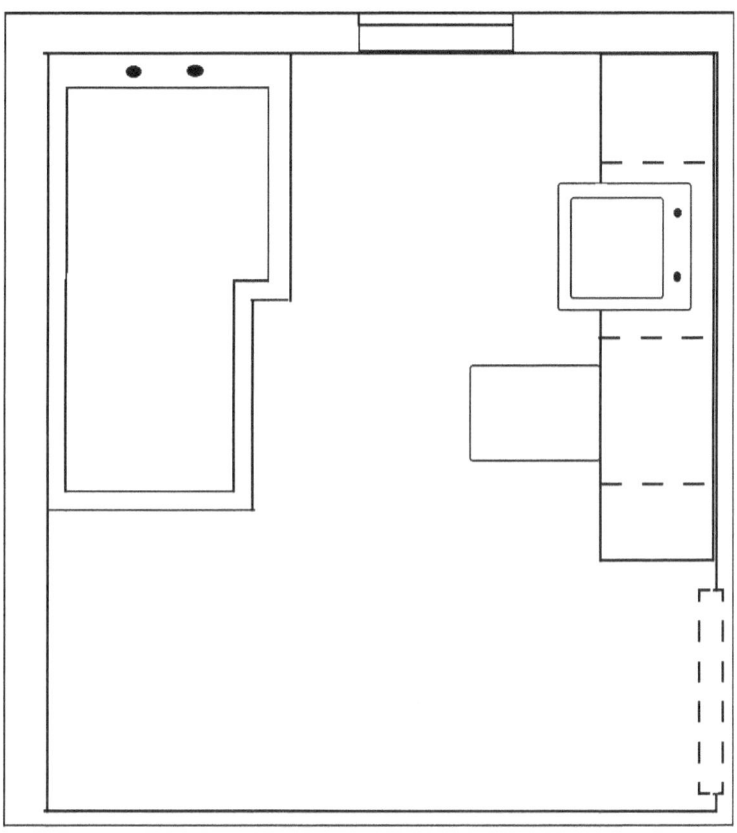

BIRD'S EYE
BATHROOM

As always bathrooms have very complex shapes and can be difficult to draw unless you lern some new techniques in shapes, but you can always present a geometric shape even if it has to be backed up with other illustrations. You are merely offering an alernative but in a credible presentation

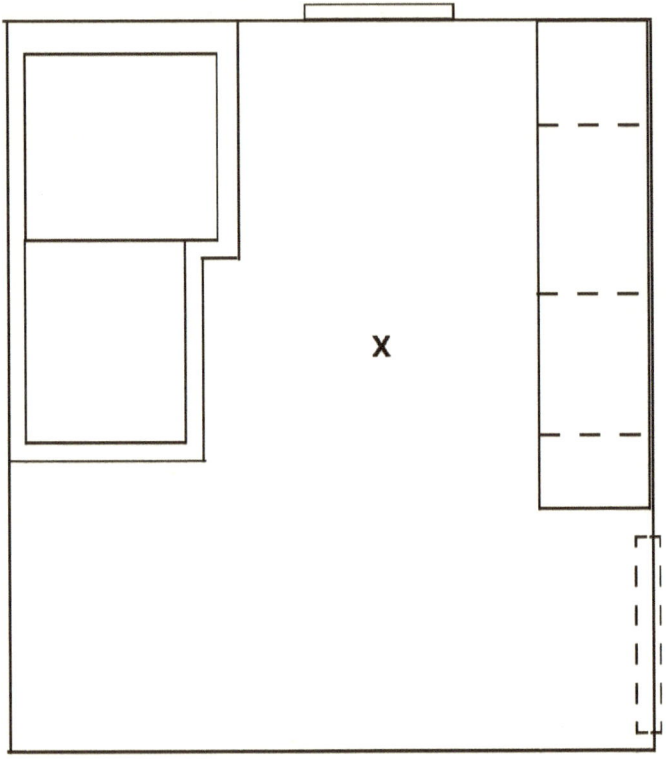

X

Strt with your
outline plan and
position your
vanishing point as
desired

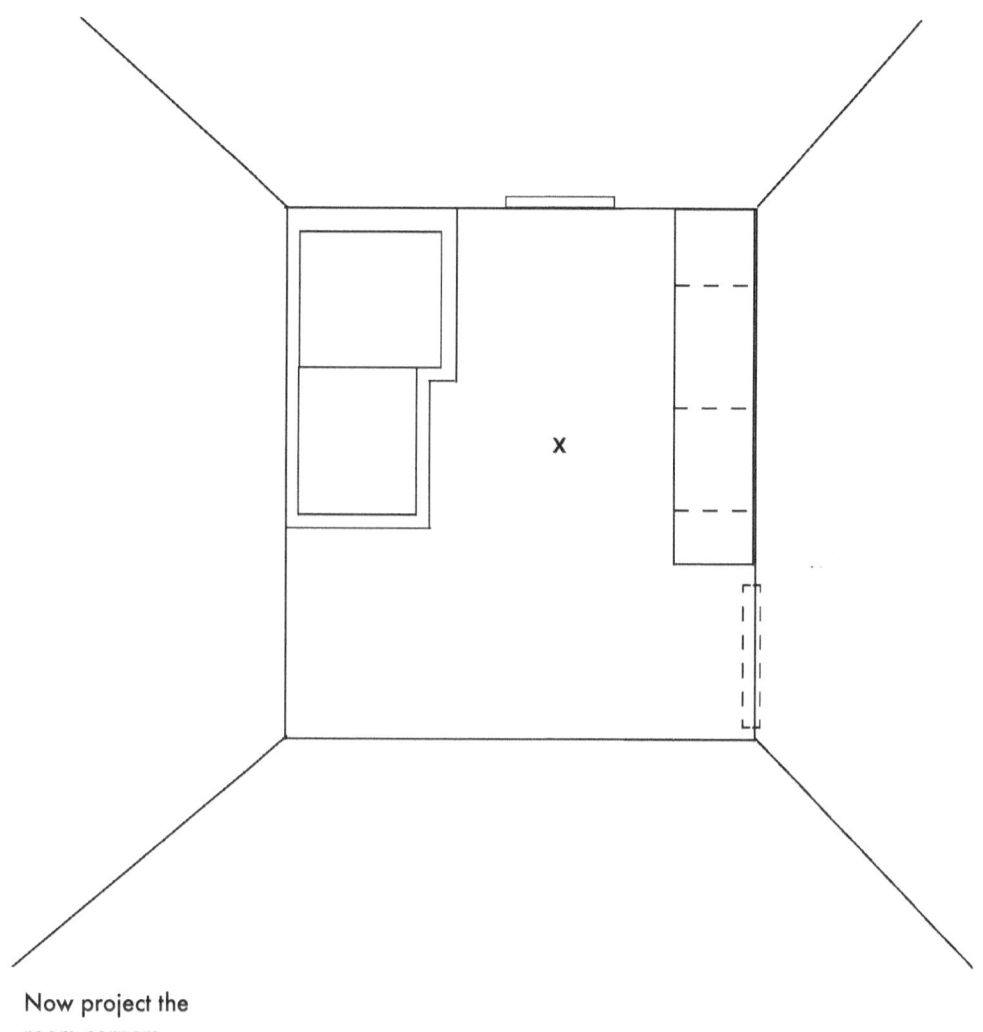

Now project the
room corners

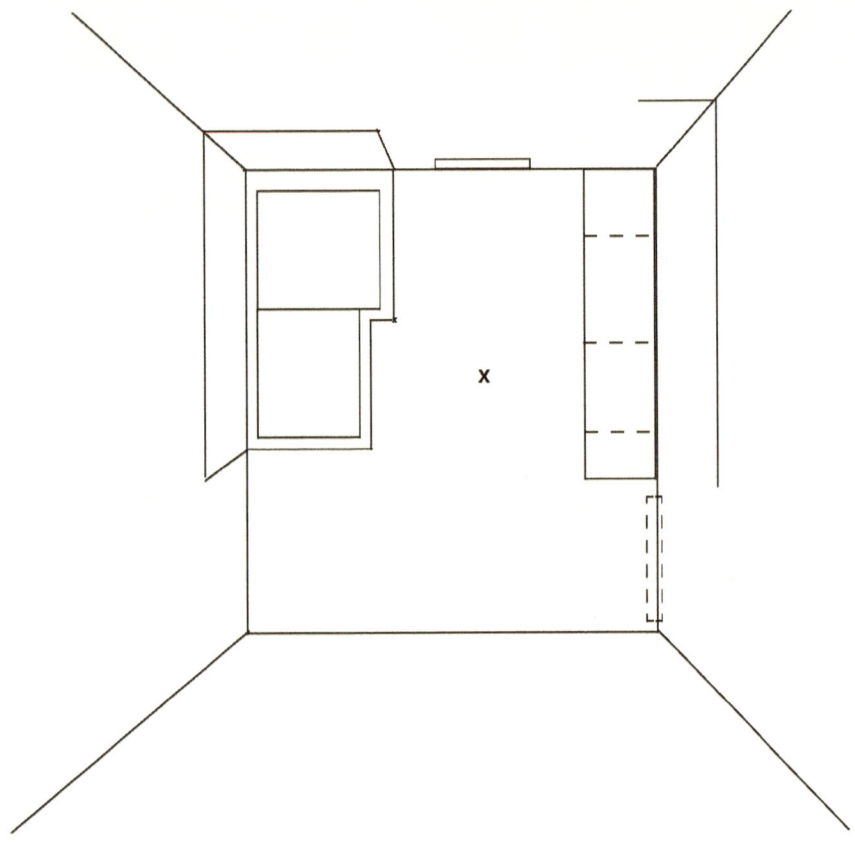

x

Start adding the
planning features

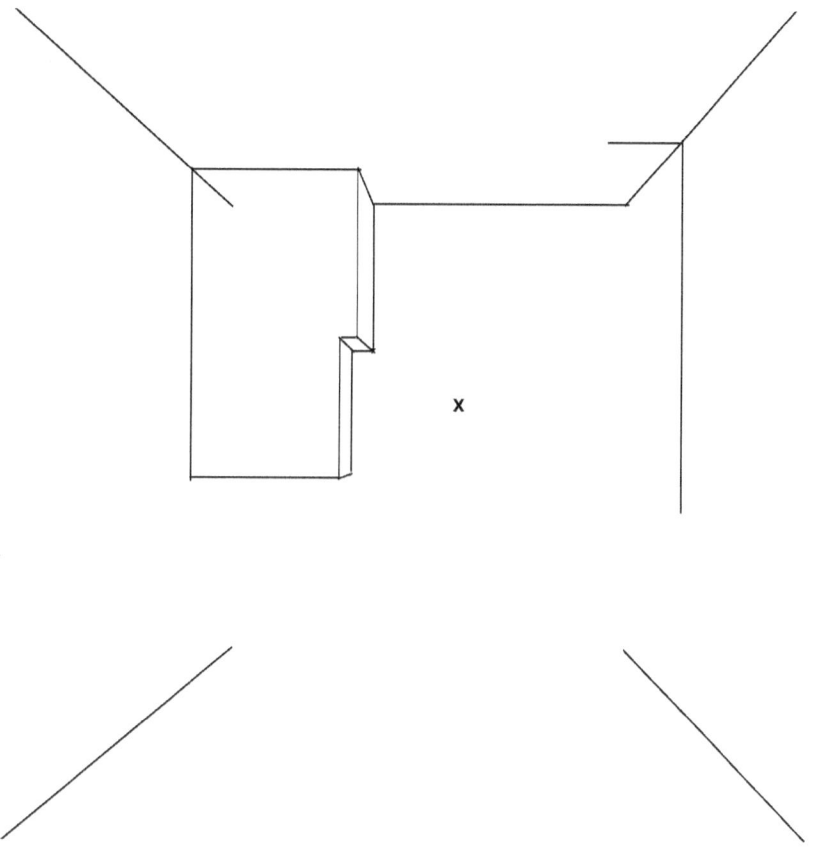

x

Now start building
the content

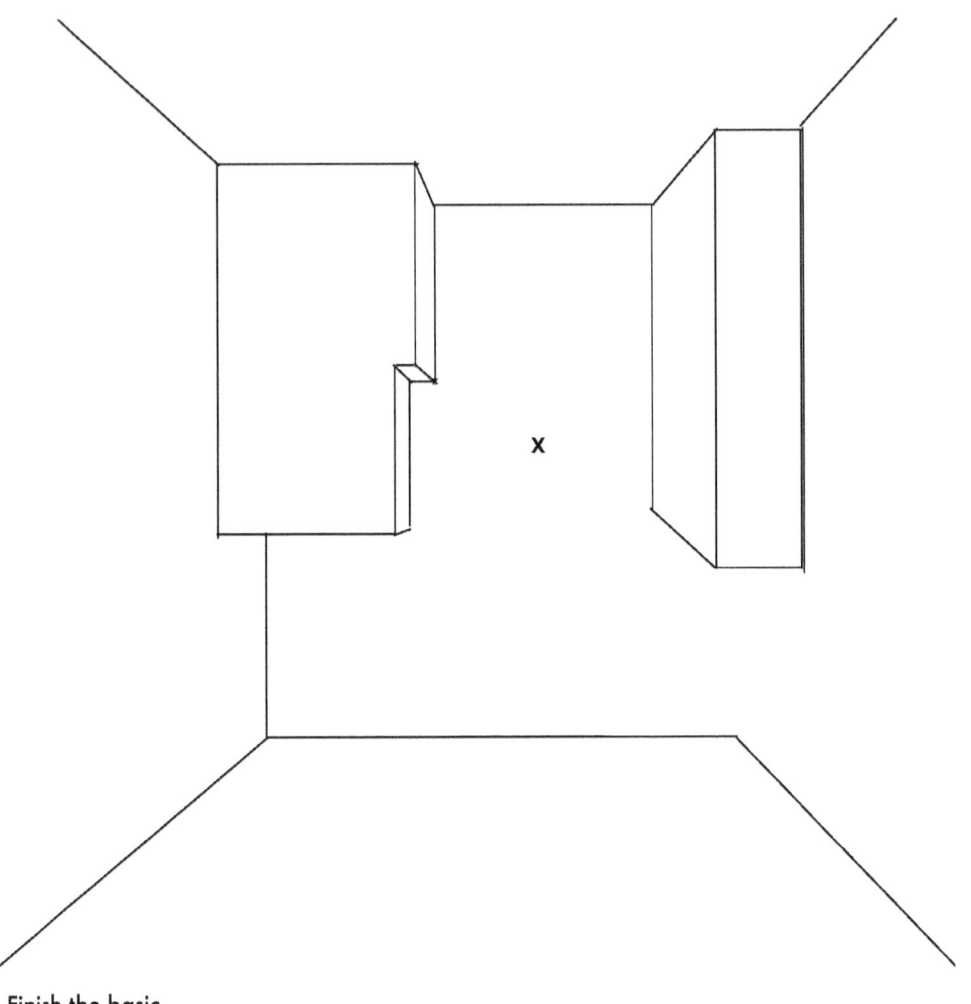

X

Finish the basic
shapes and
carcassing

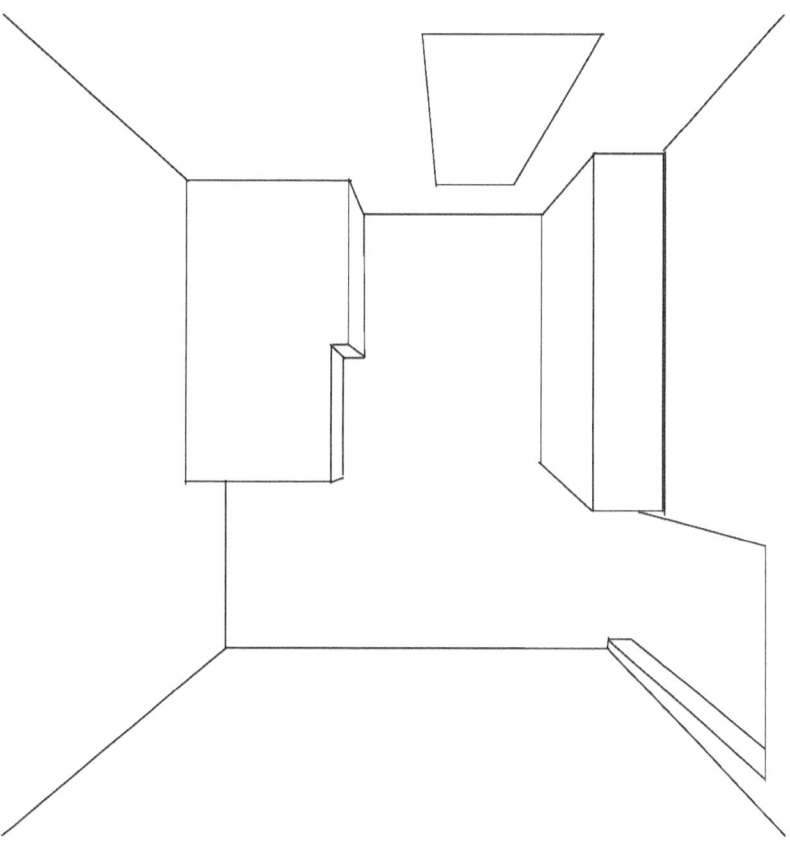

Continue with
architectural details

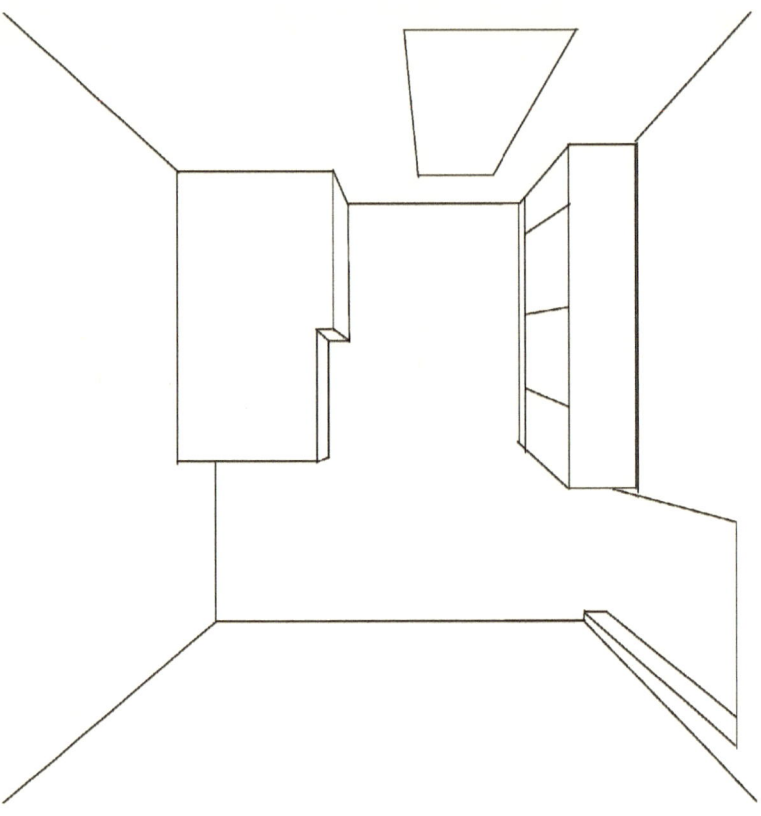

**Continue with
further details**

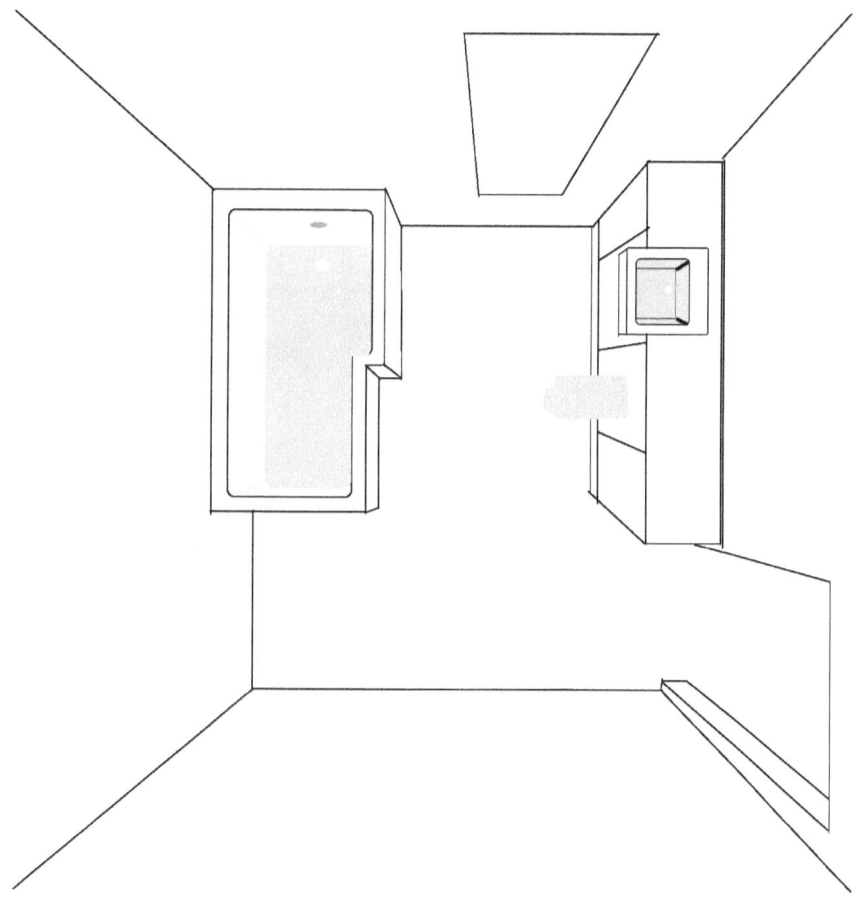

Start adding
appliance features -
shading and
ghosting can be a
useful tool

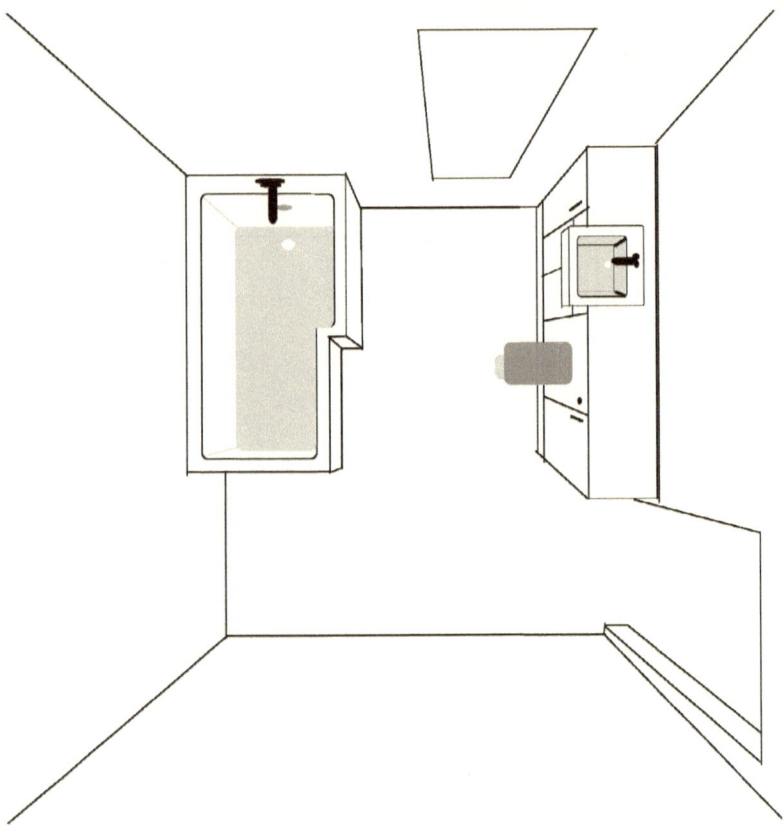

Continue detail

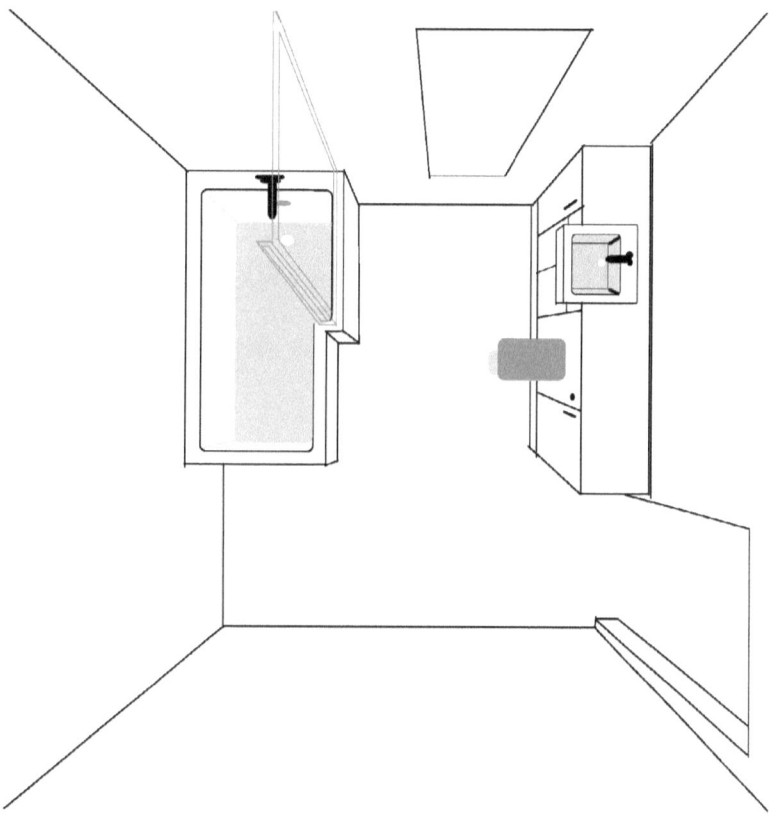

Detiling such as
shower screen

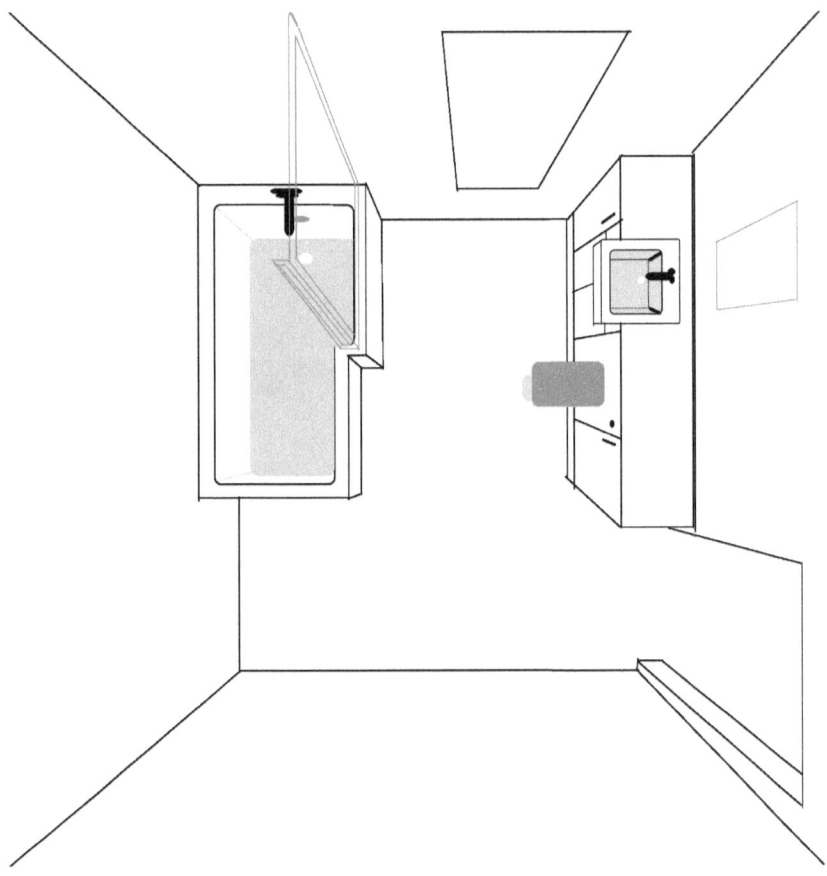

More detail

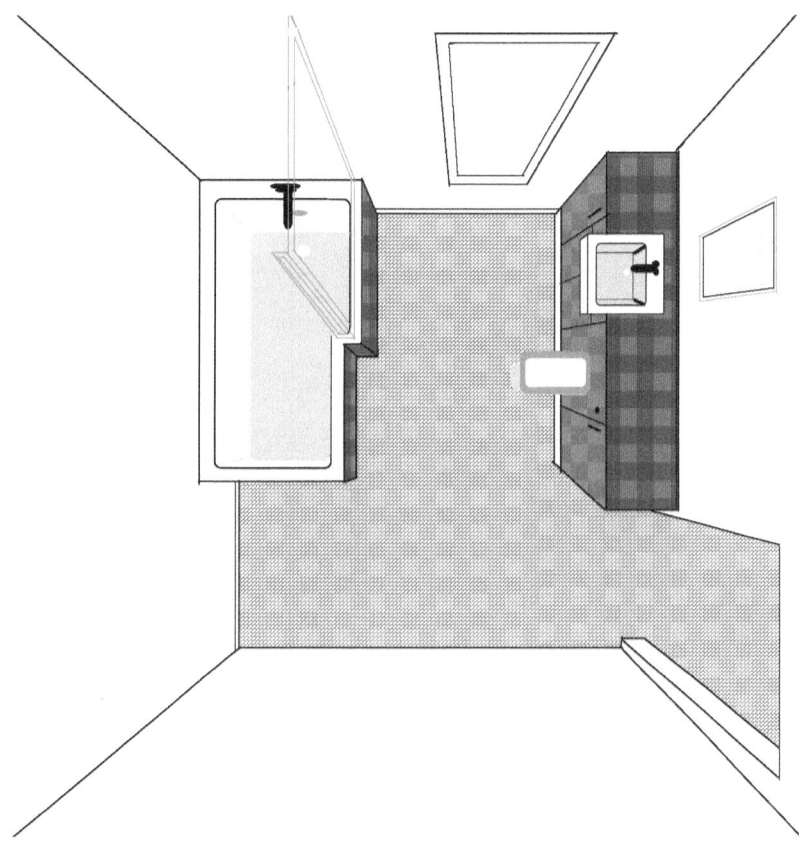

Finish detail and
shading

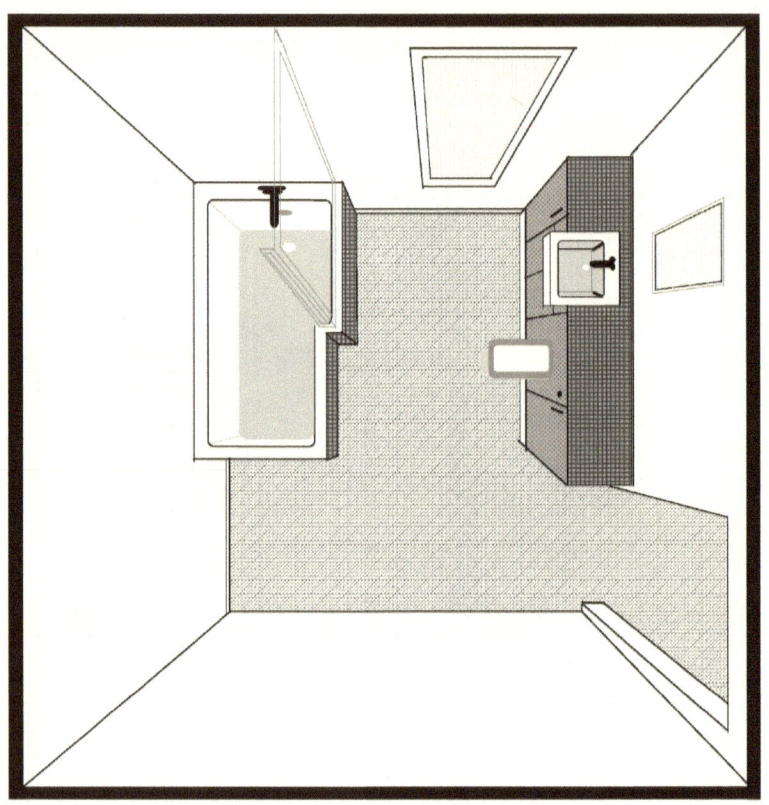

Border and rendering

Image of our
chosen bathroom

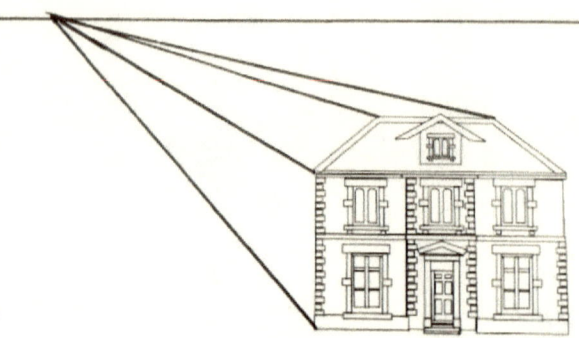

17

TRANSFORMING

This chapter is about taking a simple drawing - even a simple 3d drawing and transforming it into a 3d possibly even a startling transformation but with a minimum of time and effort.

Our fist example is the EXTERIOR 2 point drawing as shown above

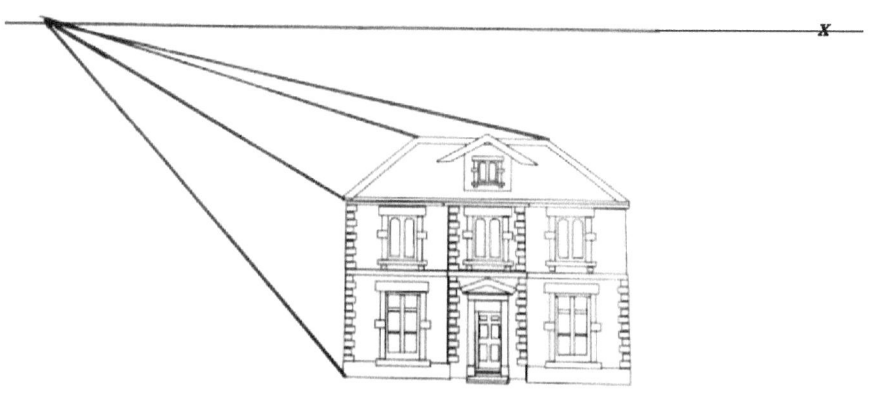

Firstly we take the
original drawing
and place a second
vanishing point on
the horizon line

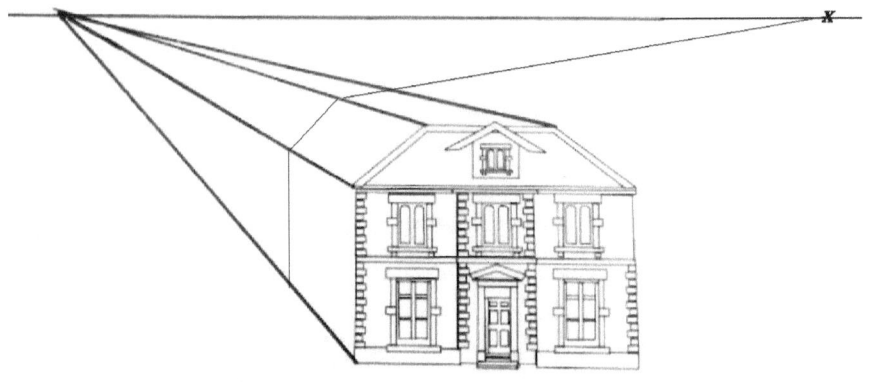

we then determine
the rear and side of
the building

outline the building
and remove some
of the original
perspective lines

Next add a bit
more interest to the
side of the building

tidy the drawing

Unfortunately it
was a hand drawn
outline not drawn
accurately but still
makes an
acceptable
presentation

We can even add
some grounds and
if you wish more
details such as
plants, ponds etc.
Total time to this
stage 10 minutes

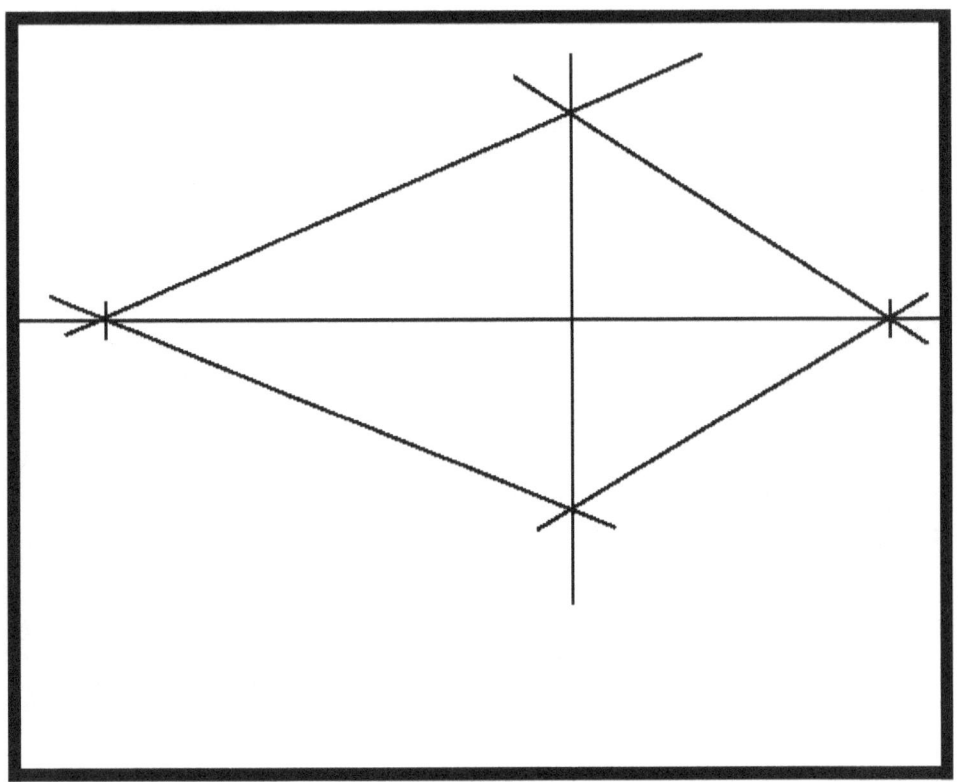

TRANSFORMING AN EXTERIOR 2 POINT PRESENTTION TO AN INTERIOR PRESENTATION

This exercise demonstrates the difference between exterior 2 point drawings and interior 2 point drawings and hopefully helps you to understand the effective differences

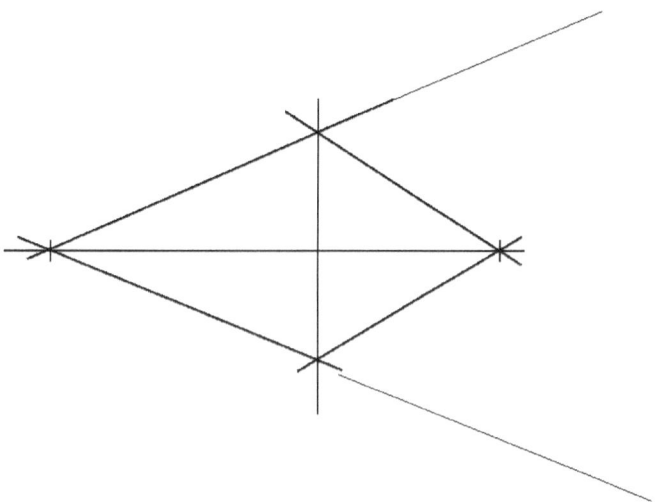

start by extending
the perspective
lines into the
opposite walls

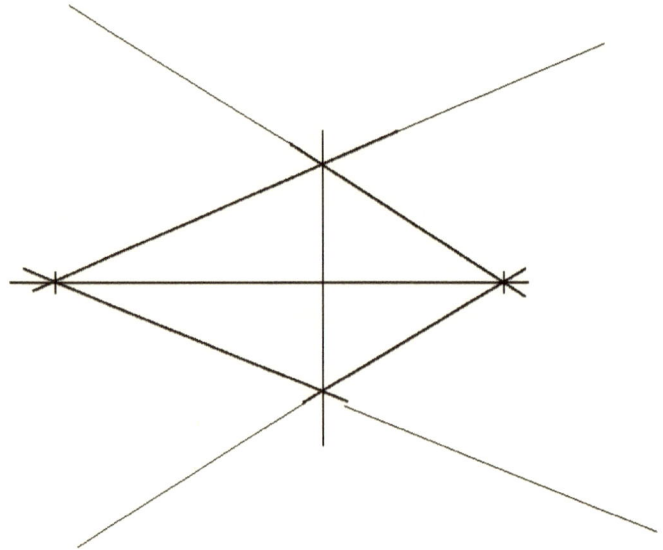

do the same both
sides

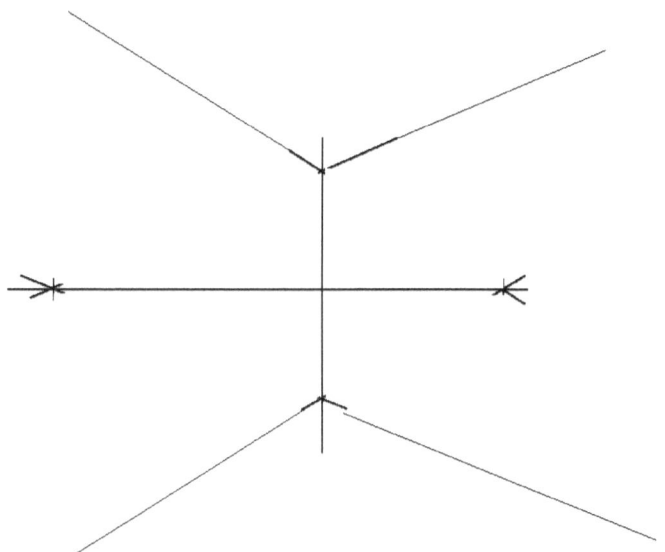

we now realize that
the vanishing points
are not far away
for effective
drawing. Interior
drawings are
obviously more
compact

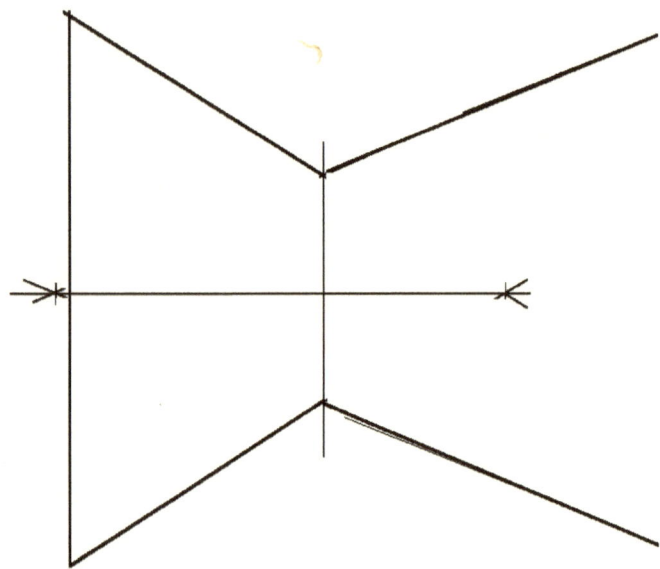

we have tidied up
the outline but still
need to work on
the VP

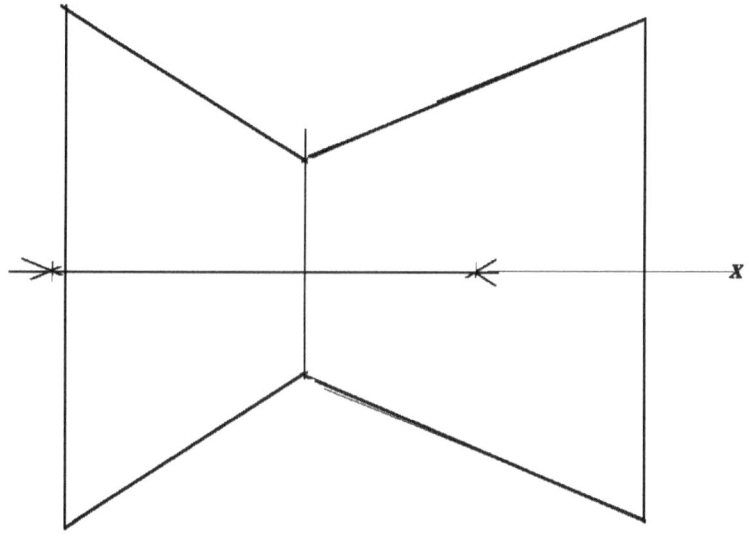

We have now moved the RH VP outside the room so we can now begin to construct our room drawing. As the VP has been repositioned it will be necessary to redraw the LH walls

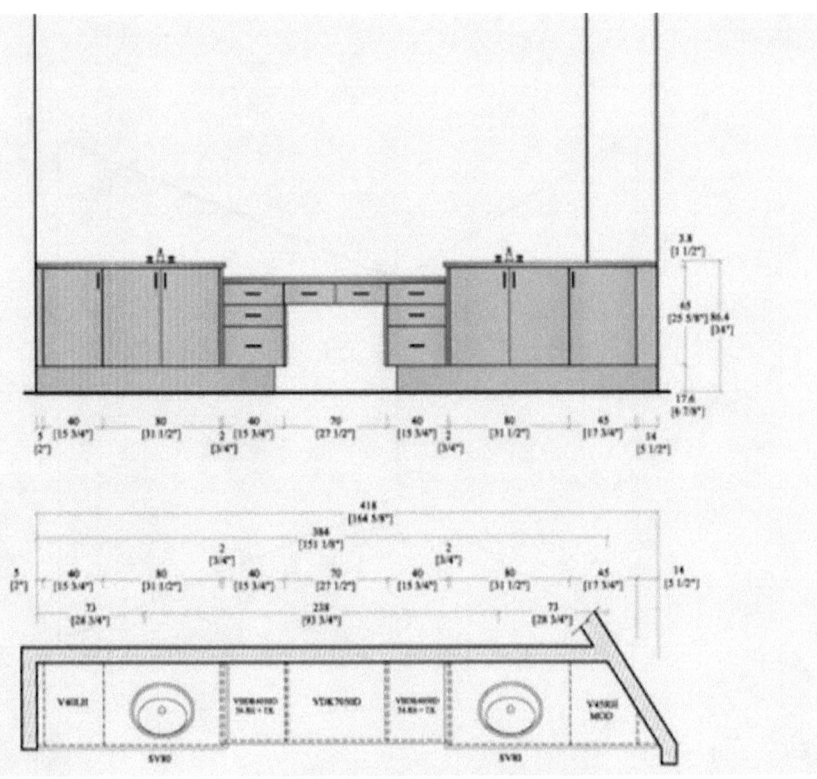

We are all used to drawing simple elevations both from a project execution viewpoint and for a sales presentation. Let's look and see how easy it is to transform such a drawing into an effective 3d presentation.

TRANSFORMING ELEVATIONS INTO 1 POINT

You may also wish to look back at our Birds Eye exercise to see how easy it is to transform a simple scale plan to 3d.

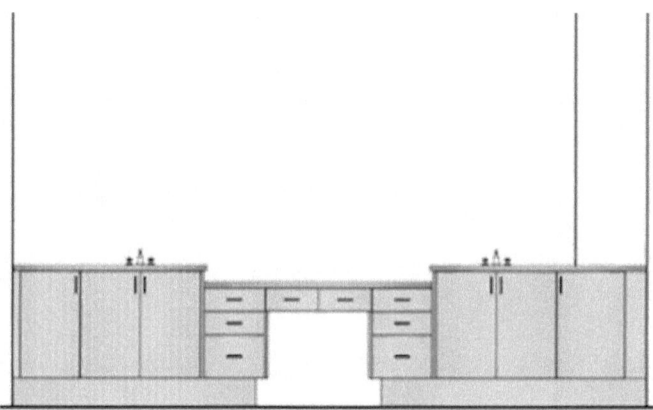

First choose a
suitable place for
the vanishing point

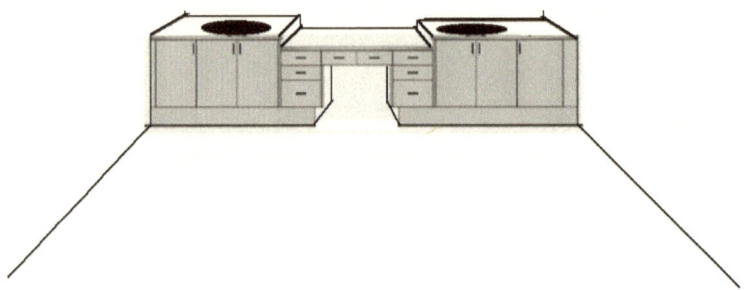

Make the drawing
come alive with
some 3d touches

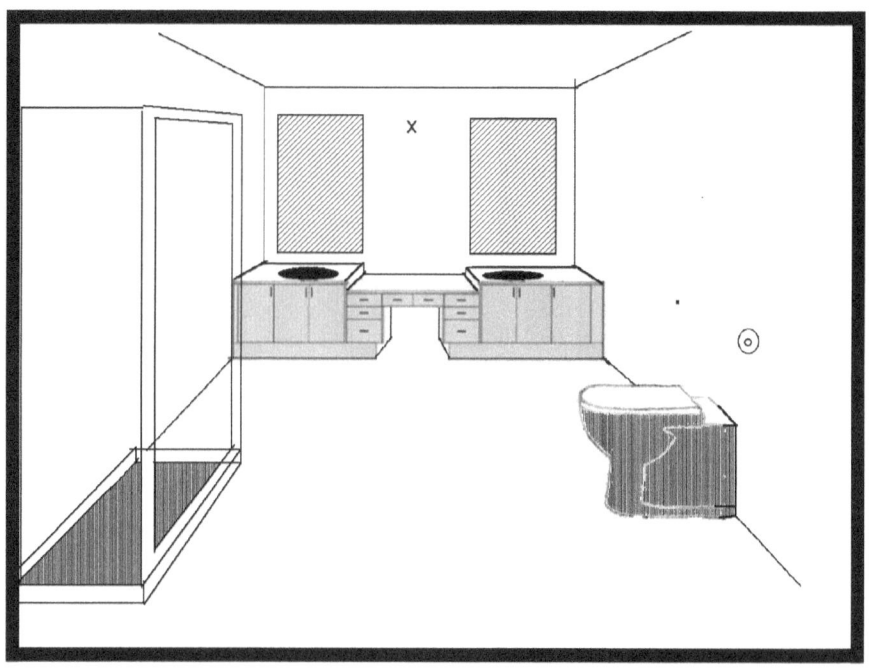

Enhance the
drawing with a
border and detail

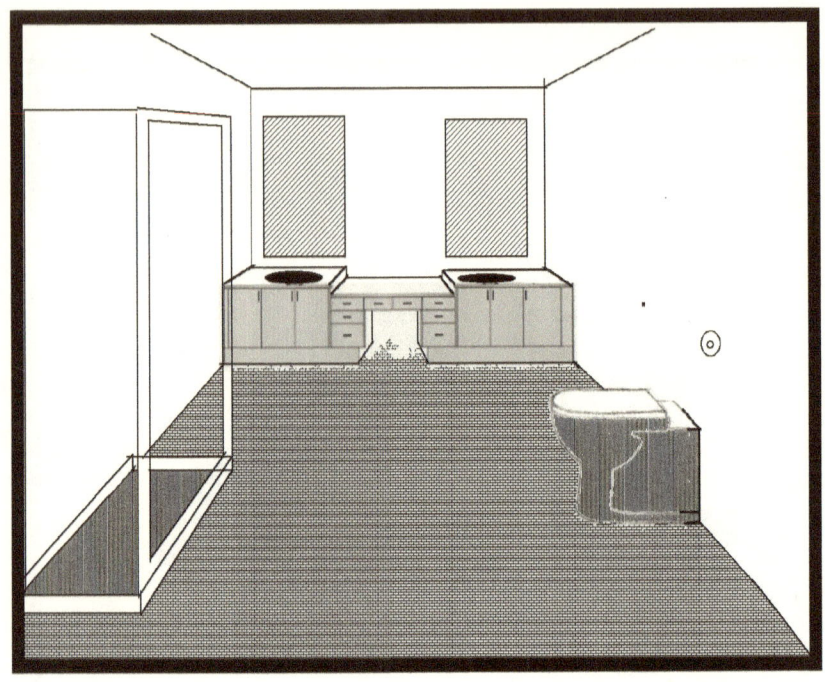

Maybe some
flooring?

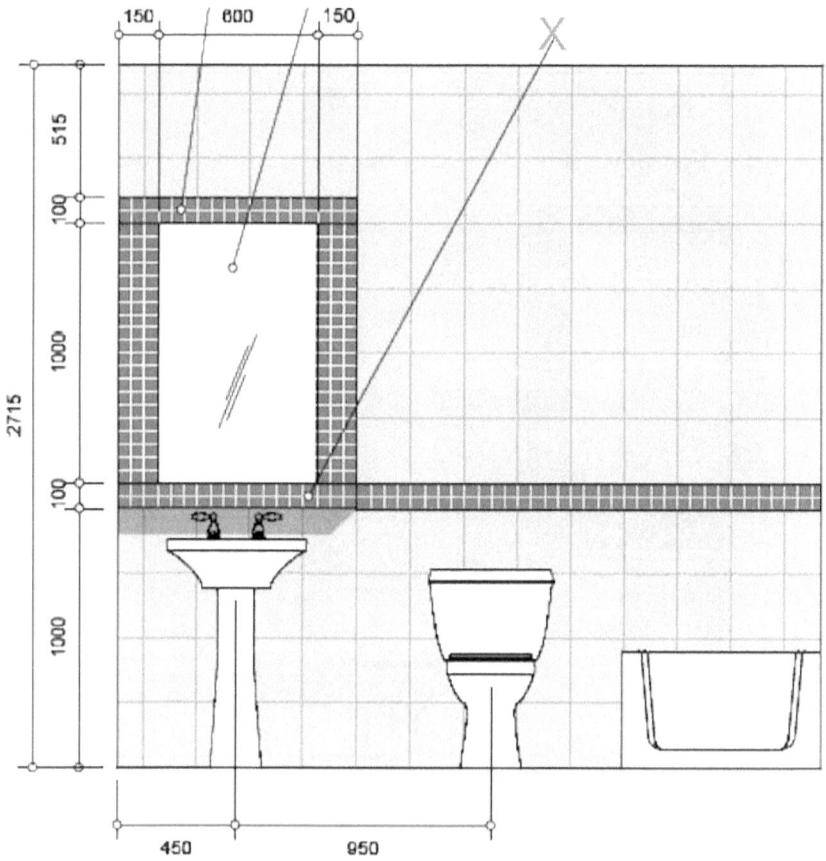

ELEVATION TO 1 POINT

This is nicely drawn elevation and serves as a decent exercise from a drawing point of view.

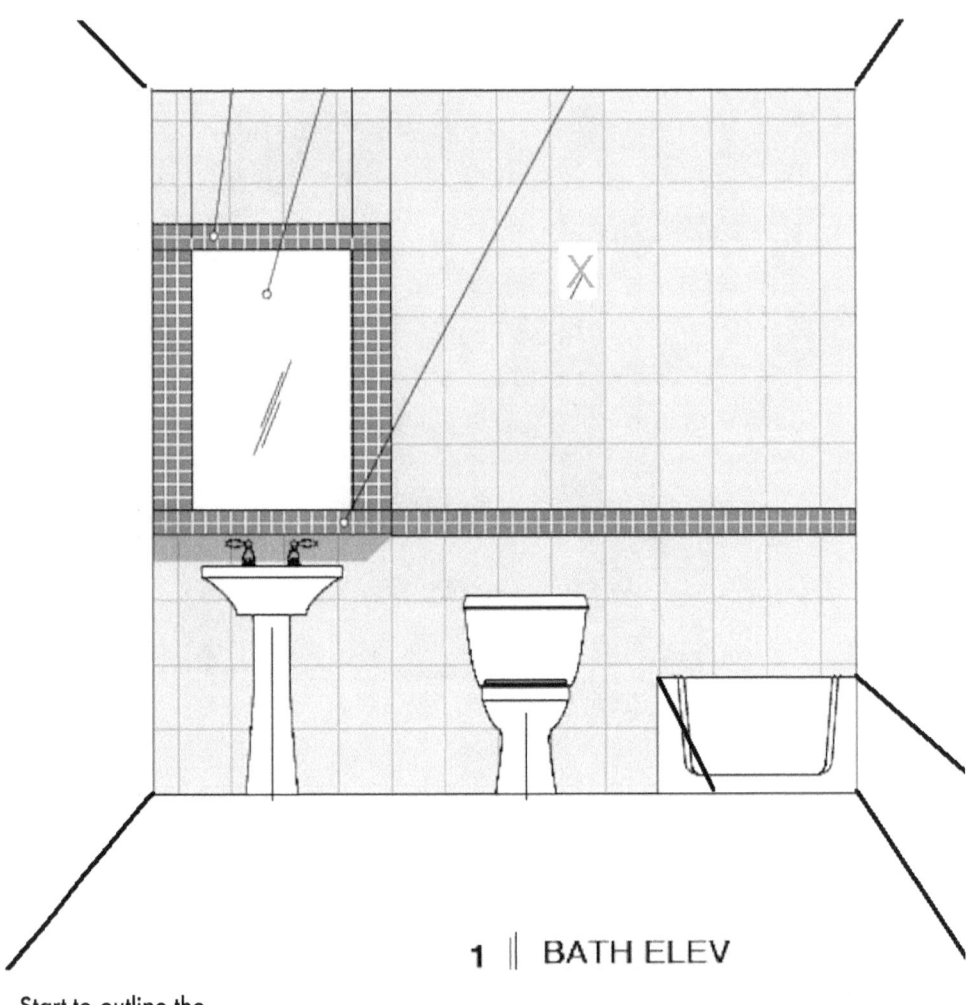

1 ‖ BATH ELEV

Start to outline the
bath and project
the walls

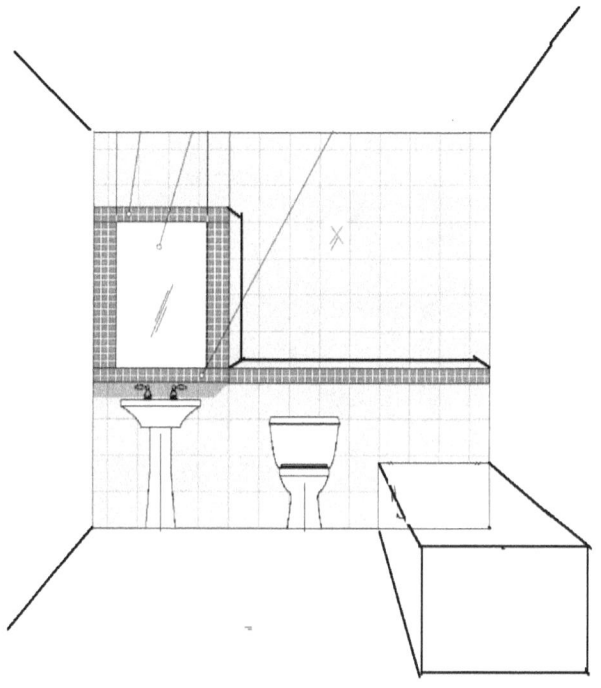

Beginning to take
3d shape

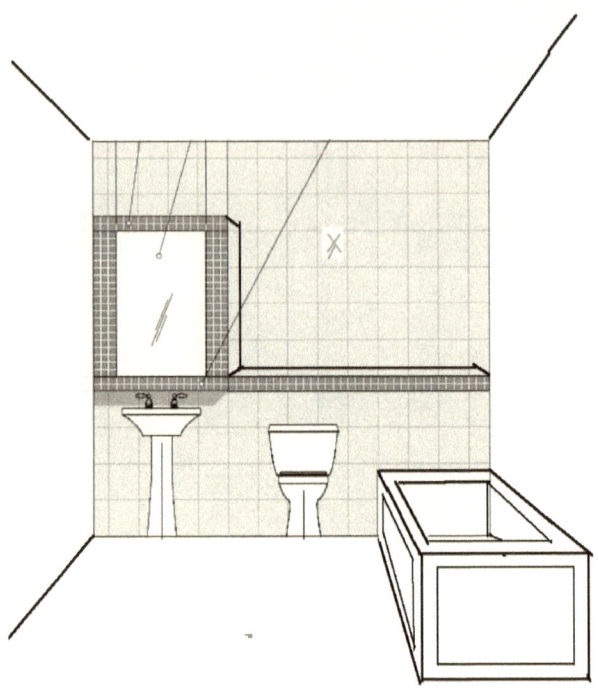

getting even better

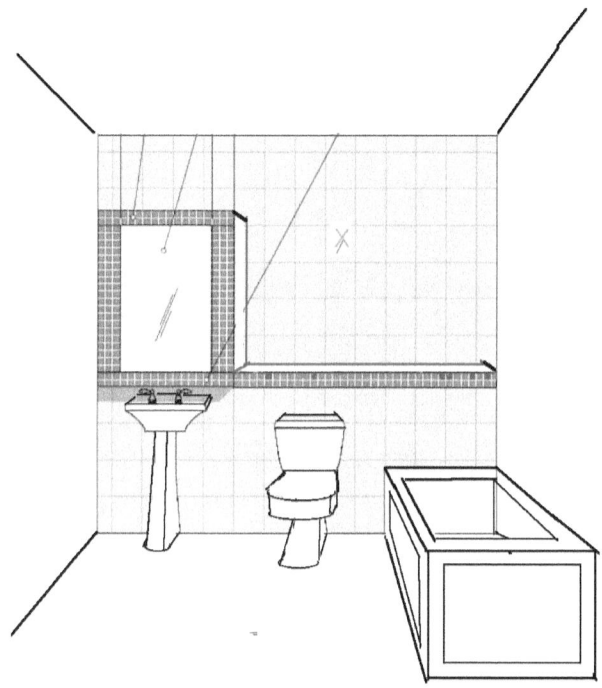

Increasing detail

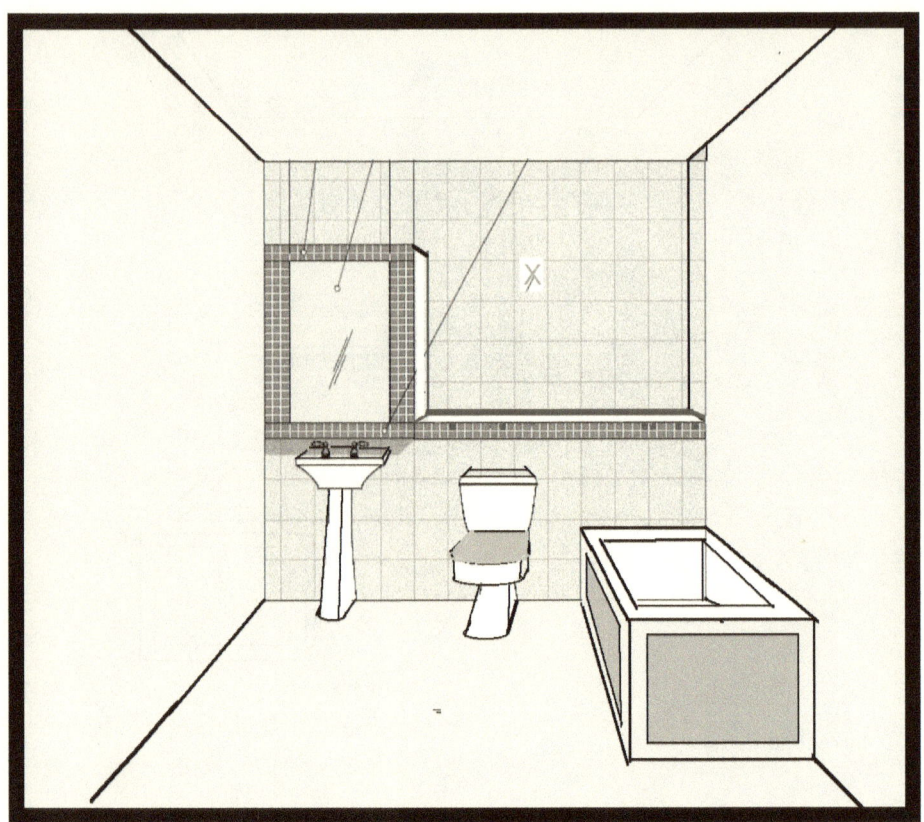

Finished?

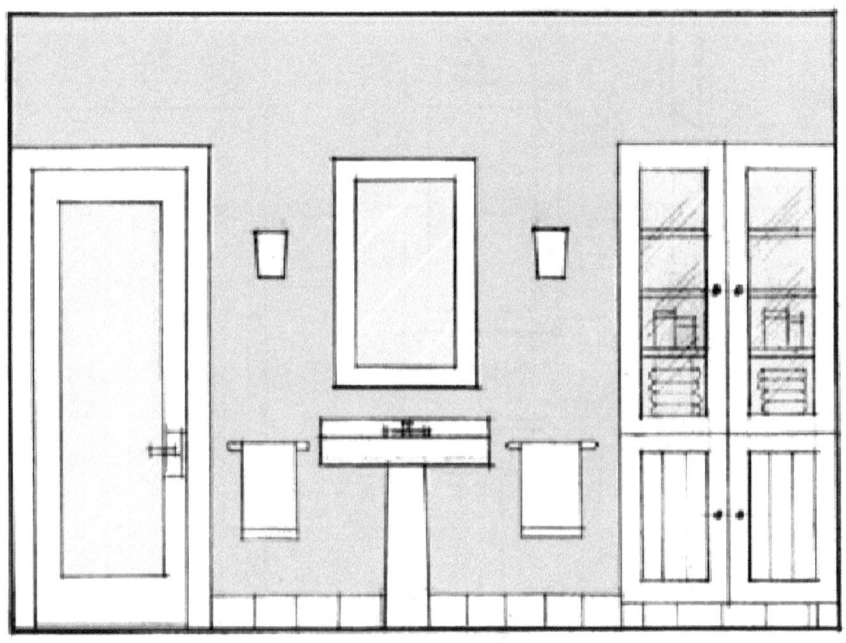

TRANSFORM ELEVATION TO 1 POINT

This is another exercise to transform an elevation to perspective: This is easily achieved in 1 POINT PERSPECTIVE: And is a very useful step in the presentation process as an elevation can be an excellent presentation tool in itself and; of course is IN SCALE.

Simply choose your
vanishing point
position and
commence
producing the 3d
effect:

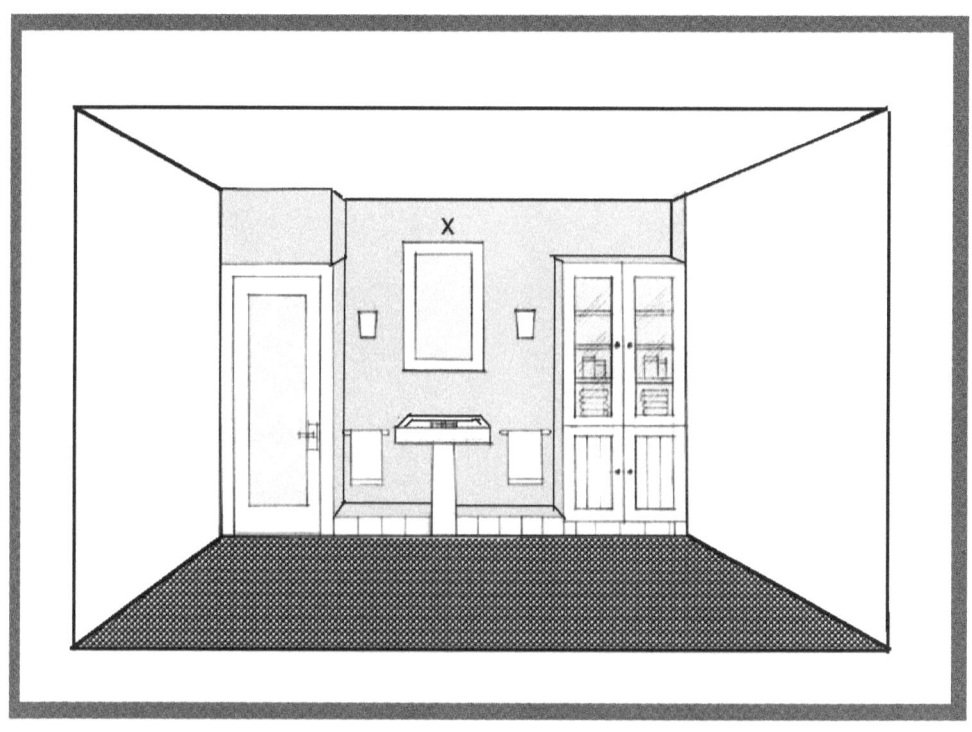

Now project the
room corners and
add a border - not
bad eh?

LITTLE BOXES

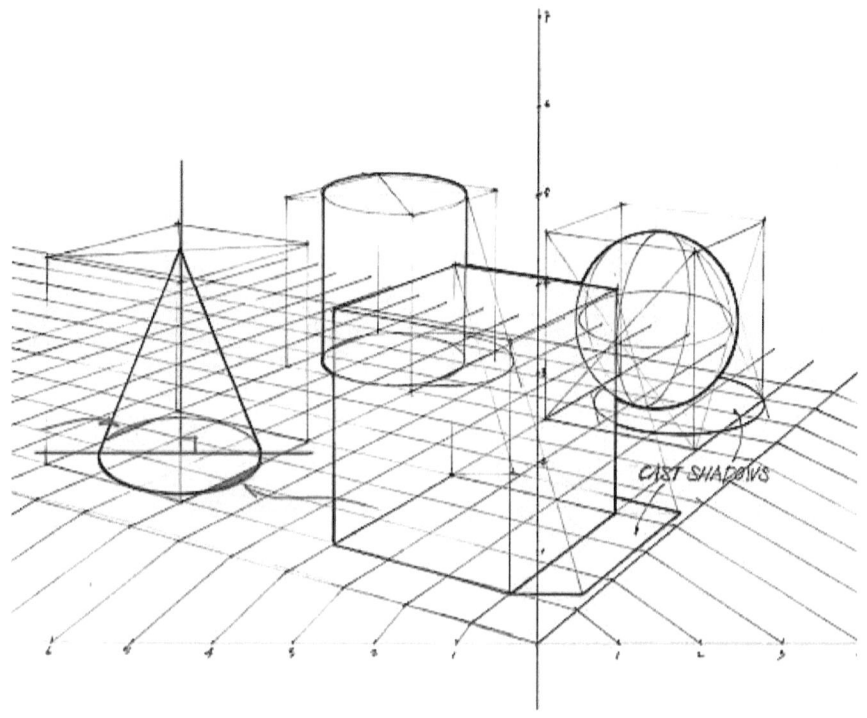

CAST SHADOWS

WHATEVER THE
SHAPE YOU ARE
SEEKING START
WITH A CUBE -
THEN SHAPE IT

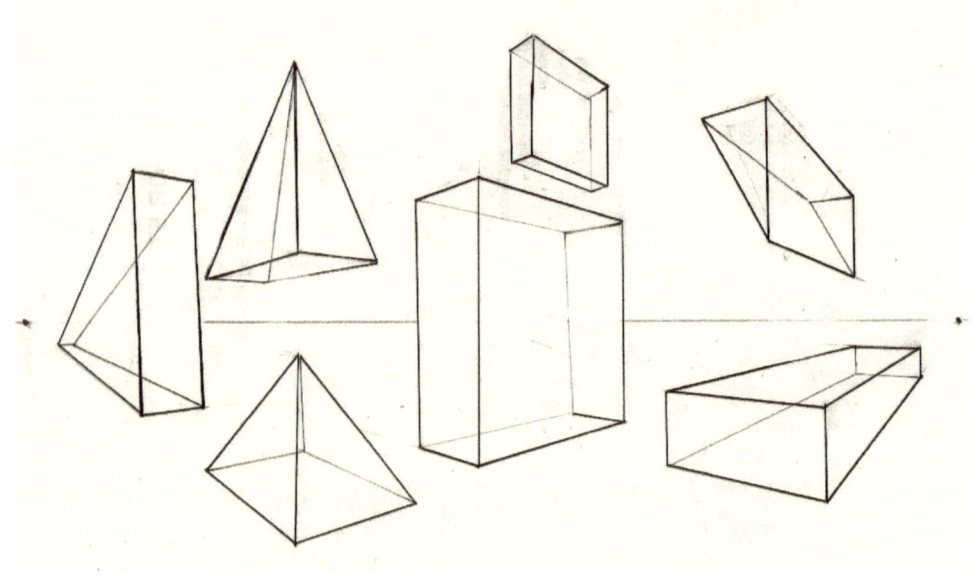

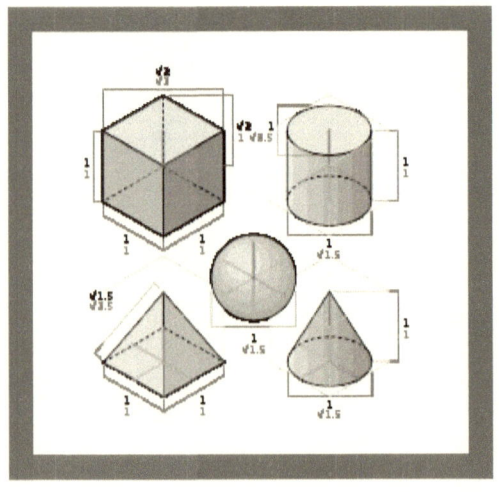

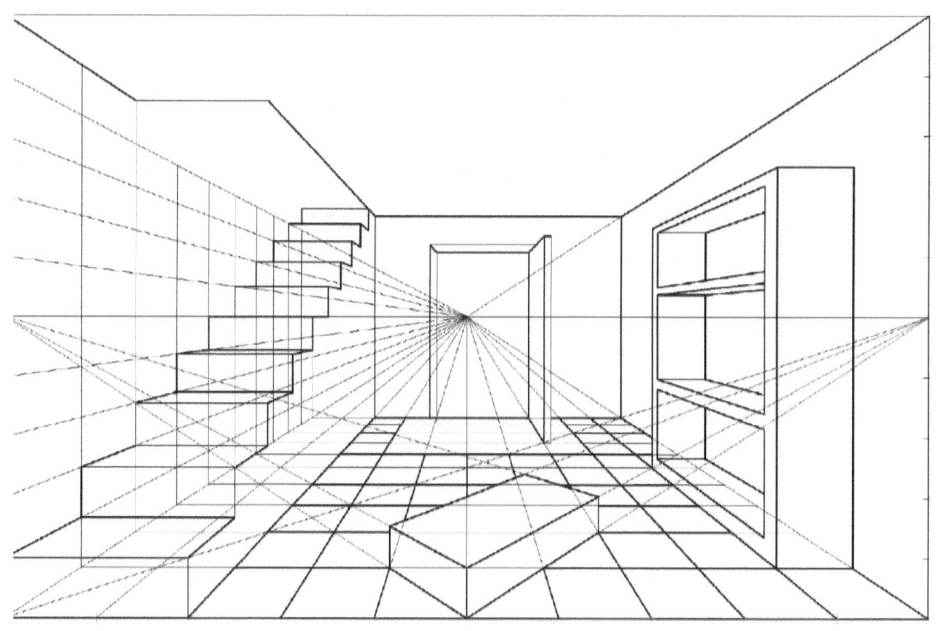

THIS IS ACTUALLY
A COMBINATION
OF 1 POINT AND
2 POINT -
interesting shapes

222

www.ingramcontent.com/pod-product-compliance
Lightning Source LLC
Chambersburg PA
CBHW030433290526
45786CB00001B/263